The Company Legal Department

The Company Legal Department

Its Role, Function and Organization

Dr. jur. Walter Kolvenbach

Attorney at Law, Düsseldorf

1979

Kluwer·Deventer·The Netherlands

Cover design: Pieter J. van der Sman

ISBN 90 312 0089 1

Contents

Preface

This study attempts to describe the role of the company law department within the company, its relation to company management and the employees who use the services of the company lawyers. It, furthermore, tries to explain that the legal advice is only one part of the operation of a legal department in a business enterprise. Other important aspects are the legal costs, organizational questions and coordination problems within the department as well as the relationship of the company legal department with the other departments in the enterprise and, last but not least, the relationship between house counsel and outside counsel.

The increasing volume of legislation and regulations in all industrialized countries resulted in an increase in the number of company legal departments and company lawyers. All large companies now have their own company legal department. Therefore, it seems appropriate to attempt to describe some aspects relating to this part of the legal profession, which is relatively new, and which has developed differently from country to country. The position of the company counsel and his relationship with the company and its employees, his professional background and his relationship with the Bar are important subjects which require further study.

Some of these problems are similar in all countries concerned; therefore, many articles published in the United States of America are also valuable for legal departments of companies in other countries. Moreover, the experiences of medium and large law firms, which have similar organizational problems or which deal with internal questions similar to those of a company legal department, can be utilized.

Based on the literature which is available and the experience of more than 25 years of work in a company legal department, I will attempt to explain some subjects which are important for company lawyers hoping that in Europe studies concerning questions of company legal departments will be initiated and encouraged. This should result in better understanding of the work of the company lawyers, their position in the company and a better organization of the work done by these departments.

I am very grateful to all my colleagues in Europe and the United States of America who encouraged me to undertake this work and who assisted me in collecting literature and cases. Without their help it would not have been possible to gather such a broad spectrum of international publications and experiences regarding this subject.

Walter Kolvenbach

Introduction

A. History of Company Legal Departments

The development of company legal departments goes back to the fourth quarter of the last century. One of the first departments was established in 1882 at Standard Oil of New Jersey.[1] Railroad companies, insurance companies and public utility companies began to employ lawyers in their business. These industries were either created by or franchised by the American States or the Federal Government. Conditions imposed in turn regulated the use of the property or franchise acquired. On the basis of these franchises and property grants the companies and their facilities spread across the country. Large numbers of lawyers were required to handle the growing number of claims and real estate cases coming up. Administrative agencies for the enforcement of new laws and ordinances forced more and more industries to employ jurists. Examples for the regulation of industries are meat inspection (1890), food and drug industry (1906) and all interstate commerce (Federal Trade Commission Act 1914).[2]

The period since 1930 has brought a great expansion of legal departments in size, number and influence. World War II brought numerous new governmental agencies. Full-time legal counsel proved to be a necessity to cope with the myriad rules, regulations and directives. Legal departments which had existed earlier grew in size and even smaller companies established their own departments.

In Europe a parallel development took place. The German Rechtsanwaltsordnung (Law regulating the Bar) of July 1, 1878, foresaw already in its § 5 that a jurist could be admitted to the Bar even if he was permanently employed by a business enterprise.[3] Industrialization and expanding economy at the end of the 19th century resulted, among other developments, in the establishment of legal departments in companies. After World War I trade unions, trade associations and large business concerns created their own legal

---

1. Quintin Johnstone and Dan Hopson, jr.: 'Lawyers and their Work − An Analysis of the Legal Profession in the United States and England', Indianapolis 1967.
2. William L. Hanaway: 'Corporate Law Departments − A New Look', The Business Lawyer, April 1962, pp. 595-602.
3. Adolf and Max Friedländer: 'Kommentar zur Rechtsanwaltsordnung' of July 1, 1878, 3. Aufl. 1930, § 5 Anm. 22.

departments and employed on a fulltime basis Rechtanwälte.[4] Since 1945 the number of jurists employed in industry and business associations in Germany also increased considerably.

The development in most other industrialized European countries is similar.

B. Literature

Beginning about 1950 a number of articles on company legal departments, house counsel and problems connected with the work of company lawyers have been published, most of them in the United States. Before 1950 the subject was almost unmentioned in the literature on the legal profession. Nearly all of the articles have been written by the heads of legal departments. The usual medium of publication is 'The Business Lawyer', a publication of the Section of Corporation, Banking und Business Law of the American Bar Association. The primary reason for these publications is to increase the understanding for the role and professional prestige of company lawyers within the legal community. They are engaged in highly important and skilled legal work. The legal department-house counsel literature is one of the most intensive efforts at operational examination by the American practicing bar.[5] Despite the size and importance of legal departments in most European companies only a few publications (especially in the Netherlands and Belgium) dealt with this phenomenon. From December 13 to 16, 1967, the 'Commission Droit et Vie des Affaires' of the University of Liège (Belgium) held a congress with approximately 200 participants to study questions concerning the company lawyer. The documents prepared for this seminar were published by the University of Liège in 1968.[6] To mention only one valuable result of this conference: In Belgium and France professional organizations of company lawyers were founded.

These examples show that also European company lawyers recognize the necessity to define their role in the business enterprise as well as in the legal profession of their country and to decide what scope their function as house counsel should have.

C. Definitions

The literature uses some terms synonymously. A brief explanation follows:

a. In Europe the English term most commonly used is *Company Legal Department* or *Company Law Department.*

4. Werner Kalsbach: 'Bundesrechtsanwaltsordnung und Richtlinien für die Ausübung des Rechtsanwaltsberufes', Köln 1960.
5. Quintin Johnstone and Dan Hopson, jr., op. cit. Page 203.
6. Le Juriste d'Entreprise − hereinafter cited as 'Le Juriste d'Entreprise'.

In the United States of America the expression more often used is *Corporate Legal Department* or *Corporate Law Department*.

It should be kept in mind that legal departments do not only exist in companies but also in business associations and trade unions. All comments made in relation to company legal departments also apply to these departments which are similarly organized and have the same problems as a company legal department.

b. Jurists working in Europe for a business enterprise as salaried employees in a legal department are called in English *Company Lawyers* or *Legal Adviser*.

In the United States the terms *Corporate Counsel, House Counsel* and *Inside Counsel* are used synonymously.

However, not every jurist employed by a business concern is a house counsel. Many employees with legal training are working in sales, personnel, and finance or as management personnel. Some of these, e.g., personnel managers, utilize part of their legal knowledge and training in their present occupation. It is possible that the company has employed them precisely, because they have a legal training. Nevertheless, they are not employed as company lawyers. House counsel, therefore, means a lawyer who is employed as a lawyer in the legal department of a business concern.[7]

c. In the United States of America the head of the legal department usually has the title *General Counsel* but also used are titles such as *Director of the Legal Department* or − especially in the United Kingdom − *Chief Legal Adviser, Legal Director* or *Legal Adviser to the Board*.

Since in the USA the head of the legal department normally is also a vice-president the complete title reads *Vice-President and General Counsel, Vice-President and Counsel, Vice-President Legal, Vice-President and Secretary-Legal.*[8]

In non-English-speaking European countries the appropriate title differs, of course, in the various countries and languages:

In the Federal Republic of Germany titles like *Chefjustitiar* or *Chefsyndikus* are frequently used; in France *Directeur du Service Juridique*.

d. Usually the lawyers in the department have a title which identifies them with the profession of law. They are designated as *Counsel, Attorney* or *Solicitor* and sometimes an adjective title which indicates their rank within the department. Typical titles of this kind are *Assistant General Counsel, Assistant Director of Legal Department, General Attorney, General Solicitor, Senior Attorney, Junior Attorney,* etc.[9]

7. William E. Brown: 'The Professional Change to House Counsel', 28, Notre Dame Lawyer, Spring 1953, pp. 333-350.
8. George W. Peak: 'Law Departments in Utility Organizations, Public Utilities Fortnightly', November 7, 1957, pp. 762-765.
9. National Industrial Conference Board Inc.: 'Corporate Legal Departments', 1950, pp. 3-31.

I. Role and Function of Company Lawyers

A. The Businessman's View of the Company Law Department

Any company lawyer will naturally regard his own department as being one of the most important management units in the company, but this is probably not the right way to look at a company law department. There are very definite expectations which management has concerning the work of a company law department and it is, therefore, not surprising that executives and heads of companies from time to time have expressed these expectations very clearly. H.B. Woodman answered the question 'What does the corporate executive expect of the corporate law department?' with the very simple words 'the impossible'. He explained in an article in 'The Business Lawyer'[1] that the corporate executive expects 'the legal department to provide competent, skilled, objective, professional legal advice and performance and, at the same time, to be an integral going part of a going business — both in the more or less truly legal activities of the department and in accepting many assignments which are essentially non-legal in nature'.

This describes already the dilemma that the company law department must be a contributing factor in the relationship of the company with customers, employees, owners, businessmen and citizens; but, on the other hand, the company lawyer is expected to maintain professional skill, integrity and, most difficult of all, objectivity. The company management expects the legal department to sell itself to the rest of the organization; to create an atmosphere where operating people want to seek its advice and services. Mr. Woodman, himself President of an American corporation, summarized the expectations for a company legal department as follows:

' 1. The corporate executive wants the legal department to be a constructive, going part of the business, contributing affirmatively to all the relationships with people that are essential to the success of the business.

2. This emphasis on the part of the corporate executive is sound and desirable, but it creates the danger of detracting from the other qualities he wants from the legal department, which are the thoroughness, competency and

1. H.B. Woodman: 'What the Executive expects of the Corporate Law Department', The Business Lawyer, April 1958, pp. 461-467.

objectivity of the professional lawyer.
3. When both the executive and the lawyer clearly recognize this built-in dilemma and make their judgements and decisions accordingly, the dual role of the lawyers ceases to be a danger and becomes a very real asset.[2]

It is certainly not by coincidence that 'The Business Lawyer' published between January 1978 and March 1978 three statements of executives concerning the role of the company law department. L. Edmund Rust, President of Southern Bell Telephone and Telegraph Company, points out that he expects the law department to provide him and the other top managers of the company with answers to legal questions upon which action can be taken. The advice has to be both professionally-sound and practical. Legal expertise has to be combined with business experience. Legal staff is to recommend courses of action. The company law department has to actively participate in the decision-making process. 'It is important to me that the general counsel be willing to volunteer his opinion in operating matters but only to the extent that it draws on his professional knowledge. In other words, I want him to keep his eye on the ball − and the ball to him is the law'.[3]
The author points out that he expects a competent law department to have experts in the special disciplines for the principal matters which emerge in the company. The department staff should not be 'yes'-men. 'The objectivity of a lawyer is his most priceless asset − and each lawyer is strictly charged to maintain that objectivity. If that objectivity were ever sacrificed simply to try to please, the advice that I and my senior colleagues would get as a result would be useless to us. Therefore, I expect the law department to define clearly and objectively for Southern Bell both what is mandatory under law and what is advisable'.[4]
Mr. Rust continues to state that the law department has to practice both preventive and representative law. Since attorneys at law are by definition of the Ethical Codes in most countries 'Officers of the Court', the members of the law department have to have a high sense of honesty and fairness. The general counsel has to be one of the 'keepers of the corporate conscience'.
The Section of Corporation, Banking and Business Law of the American Bar Association presented a program on August 9, 1977, on the subject 'A Businessman's View of Lawyers'. Panelists were a number of important businessmen, and in the discussion it came out that businessmen look upon lawyers for what one of them called 'intelligence, or early warning'.[5] Bills being debated in Washington (and the same is of course true for any other parliament in the world) have to be followed very closely by company lawyers

2. H.B. Woodman, op. cit., page 467.
3. L. Edmund Rust: 'What the Chief Executive looks for in his Corporate Law Department', The Business Lawyer, January 1978, pp. 811-815.
4. L. Edmund Rust, op. cit., page 814.
5. Donald L. Fry: 'A Businessman's View of Lawyers, A Program', The Business Lawyer, January 1978, pp. 817-845.

so that proper warning can be given to the company well ahead of time. New trends and new types of legislation are most important for any company operating in highly industrialized countries. Therefore, not only legislation for the home market, but also for export markets of the company, has to be closely followed and monitored by the legal department so that proper action can be taken by the company in good time to prepare for such new legislation and/or restrictions.

Donald L. Fry, Chairman of the Board, Bell & Howell Company, pointed out in the discussion that 'a chief executive isn't very smart if he doesn't get in touch with the general counsel early on something. If he doesn't ask counsel's legal advice and commentary on some significant action proposed early enough, he gets himself in trouble. This probably sounds obvious and too logical, but early consultation is frequently not done resulting in trouble there-after'. Mr. Fry considered it important for a chief executive to know his principal lawyers personally and deal with them no matter where they may be assigned in the organization so that he knows who and where they are and how they think and arrive at their judgements.[6]

Most of the panelists emphasized that they expect of a lawyer the special combination of technical skill and practical understanding that enables a lawyer to protect his client, but not make the deal impossible.

John D. de Butts, Chairman of the Board and Chief Executive Officer, American Telephone and Telegraph Company, also commented on 'The Client's View of the Lawyer's Proper Role'.[7] AT & T established an Executive Policy Committee 6 or 7 years ago. This committee deals with all issues of policy and is thus probably the most important management committee of the company. It is made up of the principal officers of the company (8 members) and its function is to advise the chairman with respect to issues that go further than the authority each one has. From the beginning the Vice-President − General Counsel of the company has been a full member of the Executive Policy Committee. He serves on the committee on precisely the same terms as any other member − that is, 'as a general officer of the business responsible for every aspect of it, rather than as the head of a particular department or the representative of a particular constituency. And he is free to give − indeed he does give − advice on general business matters whether they have legal implications or not'.[8]

Mr. de Butts believes that any topic of the Executive Policy Committee has at least potentially legal implications and continues: 'To put the matter another way, what makes the lawyer's advice unique, i.e. distinguishable from the advice of any of his management colleagues, is that it is just that: lawyer's advice. It reflects a commitment to standards that transcend the requirements of his particular employment, standards to which, as long as he remains a

6. Donald L. Fry, op. cit., pp. 820, 821.
7. John D. de Butts: 'The Client's View of the Lawyer's Proper Role', The Business Lawyer, March 1978, pp. 1177-1185.
8. John D. de Butts, op. cit. page 1180.

lawyer, he owes his first allegience. By being included in top level discussions that lead to the establishment of company policies, strategies and programs, the general counsel is in a position to evaluate their legal and ethical significance and to express positive opinions that can influence them'.[9] If the managers of the operating divisions of the company know that the general counsel has a voice in top management decisions, they will listen to all the lawyers in the organization before they make decisions at lower levels of management. Therefore, it is a real advantage to have the top legal officer on the executive policy committee or the Board of Directors.[10]

The chief executive officer looks to the company lawyer's advice for candor, wisdom and courage (wisdom being the same as 'practical judgement'). He wants the company lawyer to be accurate and perfect in his work. Legal opinions should be articulated in such a way that they communicate ideas briefly and in a readily understandable form. The work must be done promptly. Modern business moves at a fast pace; therefore, postponement of business decision because of delay in the legal opinion can mean irreparable loss for the company.[11]

But not only in the United States, also European heads of companies realize more and more the importance of close cooperation between top management and legal department. Businessmen recognise that the training of jurists can have many advantages for business life, regardless whether the jurists works as a lawyer in the company or in a non-legal managerial position. Dr. Max Gloor, one of the managing directors of the Nestle-Group, who was at one time himself a company lawyer, lists the following advantages of jurist-managers:

− He states facts objectively. He has learned to differentiate between important and less important facts.
− Closely connected with the ability to describe the facts is the gift not to get lost in details. He has learned to subordinate the individual case to the overall strategy.
− He has been trained to look ahead into the future and thus to recognise the various possibilities which the realization of a commercial transaction might necessitate.
− The jurist has been trained to think logically and methodically, to concentrate upon a problem and to bring it to a conclusion.
− He knows that often for one problem not only one opinion or one solution exists. Therefore, he is used to consider also other opinions and discuss problems with others and only, thereafter, draw his own conclusions. This furthers teamwork which is most important in business.
− The jurist knows the technique of negotiation and, therefore, also the

9. John D. de Butts, op. cit. page 1180, 1181.
10. 'Ethical Responsibilities of Corporate Lawyers', The Business Lawyer, Special Issue, March 1978.
11. J.H. Binger: 'What I expect from the ideal Corporate Counsel', The Business Lawyer, April 1966, pp. 836-842.

technique to conclude agreements.
- He is open for innovations because the legal world is changing rapidly and he has to deal with new regulations and facts all the time.
- The jurist does not avoid to make decisions because he has been trained to make decisions every day.[12]

I would like to quote a statement made by an English top manager, M.R. Mathys, who as businessman asks the company lawyer:

- 'Please understand my situation − it is so frequently black or white; I either put up the plant or I do not; I either make profits or I am out; I have to balance the pros en cons, so please do all the reasoning but keep it to yourself and tell me the conclusion as positively as possible.
- Please keep a sense of proportion and have regard to the nature and size of my business and put your major effort into those matters which will have a substantial impact on my business.
- Please try to get the priorities right.'[13]

One of the most affectionate statements concerning the general counsel was made by the chief executive officer of one of the largest German companies: in an address he pointed out that in former times the most important person in the entourage of royalty was the physician who was responsible for the health of the prince. In modern times great responsibility rests upon the top managers of large companies and the most important person they have to work with is the general counsel. They permanently require his professional advice in order not to become entangled in the intricacies of modern legislation and regulations.

I have intentionally quoted some statements of important American chief executive officers because they show that the role of the general counsel and the company law department in the USA is much stronger than it is in almost all European countries. A survey of the conditions existing in European countries shows that the company lawyer is regarded as necessary but that he is not always, or even frequently, involved in the decision-making process at the highest level of the company. European companies only too often believe that the head of their legal department is a specialist, who does not have to be a member of the management board of the company.

A top management which responds positively to the idea of legality for business enterprises will classify its chief lawyer in a high hierarchical position because it wants to make sure that the legal component of a decision is made at the same level as the other components, i.e. financial, commercial, technical, etc. The role which the company lawyer has to play in the decision-making process cannot be based only upon the value of his personality, but rather he must have the same hierarchical level as his colleagues who have supreme

12. Dr. Max Gloor: 'Der Jurist im Wirtschaftsleben' Schweizerische Juristen-Zeitung, April 1963, no. 7 und 8.
13. M.R. Mathys: 'Lawyers and Businessmen', Le Juriste d'Entreprise, pp. 337-344.

responsibility in other functions involved.[14]

A study made in 1969 showed that in the United States of America in companies employing fewer than 5,000 people and in those with more than 25,000 employees, the predominant practice is to have the chief legal officer report directly to the chief executive officer or the chief operating officer.[15]

The chief executive officer who places his chief company lawyer in a hierarchical position of equality with the top managers responsible for the other decision components will look upon him as a true adviser and not only as an assistant for the execution of legalities. A precondition is, of course, full and unlimited confidence not only in his legal qualifications and his secrecy but also in his loyalty. If that is the case, his critique and opposition based on professional judgement will not only be properly valued and understood but even asked for. The company lawyer must convince his colleagues that he abides by and interprets the law objectively and that the sentence 'The law is what is profitable for the enterprise' is not his credo.[16]

If the work of the company lawyer is considered to be of only marginal importance, a kind of insurance against accidents, or if he is regarded as a kind of company fire brigade for the removal of break-downs, then the words of Martin Luther can rightly be applied: 'Der Jurist, der nichts ist als ein Jurist, ist ein arm Ding' (Translation: 'The Jurist who is nothing but a Jurist is a poor fellow').

The complexity of our economic life and its dependence upon government regulations and legislation even in the most liberal countries make it mandatory for management to have legal advisers participating in every phase of the decision-making process. It, therefore, can only be hoped that the experiences which the large US corporations have made will no longer be neglected by their European competitors.

B. The Role of the Company Lawyer

The high expectations expressed by top managers of large companies bring up the question of the company lawyer's role in a business organization environment.

In order to answer this question it is necessary to look first at the opinion which the public has of the lawyer as a professional. The lawyer is a man of great independence who normally, and in most countries until today, practices alone or with a very limited number of partners. He is a member of a profession which has among others the following characteristics:

---

14. Xavier de Mello: 'L'Association Francaise des Juristes d'Entreprise et le Juriste d'Entreprise', mimeographed, 1977.
15. R.E. Gorman and James K. Brown: 'Legal Organization in the Manufacturing Corporation', The Conference Board Record, August 1969, pp. 42-47.
16. G. Prost: 'Der Jurist in der Wirtschaft' Neue Juristische Wochenschrift 1967, pp. 17-21.

'1. Expertise in the use of a body of specialized knowledge;
2. Control through voluntary associations of those practicing the profession and through the internalization of the norms or rules of the profession (usually expressed in a formal code of ethics learned over a long period of training);
3. Action taken in conformity with universal standards based on the body of specialized knowledge;
4. Impersonality in dealing with the client;
5. Professional status achieved by performance;
6. Elimination of self-interest in professional decisions.'[17]

But, the law − at least as practiced at the upper levels of the blue-ship bar − is not only a profession but a discipline, 'a pattern of thinking, an ability to assimilate information, a capacity of switching from one subject to another, all the while combining the patience of the psychiatrist and the passion of the preacher'.[18]

In the practice of any profession, service comes first while the operation of a business organization is primarily profit oriented and service is only one way to this end. Because of the technical intricacies of professional work, there must be a strong reliance on personal motivation and a large degree of autonomy in the details of work. For lawyers the ideals of professionalism are widely accepted. [19]

Max Weber, the German sociologist, has defined and described the logics of large organizations by listing the following characteristics:

1. Specialization of function, which promotes expertise on the part of the administrator;
2. Hierarchical authority structure, in which the administrator of each level has clearly defined authority over his subordinates and is responsible for their actions to his superior;
3. A formally established system of procedures, rules and regulations governing the decisions and actions of the administrators which, with the authority system, promotes coordination and uniformity of decision and operation;
4. Impersonality in official action through the application of the procedures and rules rather than through personal involvement with others in the organization or with its clients;
5. Appointment to positions in the organization based on technical qualifications, with employment considered a full-time career.[20]

17. Peter M. Blou and B. Richard Scott: 'Formal Organizations, A Comparative Approach' 1962, pp. 60-63.
18. Paul Hoffmann: 'Lions in the Street', The Inside Story of the Great Wall Street Law Firms, 1973, p. 37.
19. Dietrich Rueschemeyer: 'Lawyers and their Society', Cambridge, Mass., 1973, p. 15.
20. Peter M. Blou and B. Richard Scott, op. cit., pp. 32-36.

Is there a conflict between profession and organization? The business organization is controlled through the hierarchy of authority and in addition formal rules and regulations which normally are developed in the organization itself. Much of the training of the personnel takes place within the organization. The profession is largely trained by representatives of its own profession and through associations, e.g. the Bar Associations. It establishes and enforces norms and standards by which the members have to abide. Thus, the member is taught to practice as an individual. In groups he practices normally only with members of his own profession which results in an association of equals. The responsibilities as an 'officer of the court' (or under German Ethical Rules "Organ der Rechtspflege") limit the loyalty toward his client. A delicate balance of commitments and duties is the result.[21] This is especially true for company lawyers who have a much closer contact with their 'client': the company and its management. Professional loyalty and obligations on one side and the loyalty to the company or individuals in the company on the other side can be very difficult to reconcile and it requires sometimes a high degree of diplomacy and character to convince the client of the necessity to observe the legal requirements.

Since a legal problem is only very seldom restricted to itself but normally arises out of its relationship with other matters, it is difficult for a company attorney to draw a clear line between legal and non-legal activities. This can result in problems for the attorney because of the codes of professional responsibility which he has to observe. The U.S. code compels the attorney not to participate in proceedings or actions which could be inconsistent 'with the fair administration of justice'.[22] Similar rules exist in most other countries. The company attorney is a member of a profession which has to uphold the law and, at the same time, an employee of a profit-seeking corporation. He can face a conflicting situation when profit and compliance with the law do not follow the same route. John D. Donnell has published a role study of 'The Corporate Counsel',[23] and in this most interesting study Professor Donnell has listed a number of areas where conflicts over the company attorney's role within the business enterprise could exist. These areas are:

1. The extent to which a corporate counsel should concern himself with business problems;
2. The authority of the law department;
3. The responsibility of counsel to serve as 'keeper of the corporate conscience';
4. How early counsel should be consulted by clients;
5. Use by counsel of his own sources of information;
6. The extent to which counsel should inform his clients' superior;

21. René Carton de Tournai: 'Les responsabilités du Juriste d'Entreprise dans la Société', Journal des Tribunaux, 13 January 1968, pp. 17-24.
22. Ethical Consideration 8 − 5 of the Code of Professional Responsibility of the American Bar Association, adopted in August 1969.
23. John D. Donnell: 'The Corporate Counsel' − A Role Study, Indiana University, 1970.

7. The desired site of the interactions between counsel and client'.[24]

Of these possible areas of conflict, number one is probably the most difficult to solve. This problem exists in all companies with law departments. The conflict results from the fact that the company lawyer deals with business problems in order to assess their legal implications. Business and legal aspects of a problem are closely connected and in most cases are impossible to separate. Therefore, businessmen have the feeling that the attorney should not give advice or make decisions in business matters, even if the attorney could make a valuable contribution to the business matter. The adverse opinions on this subject can probably best be described by two answers of business executives which Professor Donnell reports: 'I'm running my business and my lawyer is just a technician'. Or even worse a statement, which Sir Henry Deterding is supposed to have made: 'I hate to see a lawyer in our office'. The opposite opinion of another businessman is: 'A legal mind is usually a very logical, methodical, incisive, analytical type of mind, so I often talk with our counsel about strictly non-legal problems relating to the business.'[25]

This shows more clearly than scientific explanations the two adverse points of view which can be found in the business community regarding involvement of company lawyers in business matters. The situation, of course, will differ in each company depending on the personalities involved − the business-man's, as well as the company lawyer's. But it depends also to some extent on the legal situation existing in the various countries. In England solicitors in permanent employment represent the company inside and outside of formal proceedings. Therefore, company lawyers often do not regard them-selves as part of management. The legal department 'is one step away' and a sharp differentiation between legal advice and management decision is noticed. The professional responsibility must prevail. For this reason in some companies members of the legal department decline to take on membership in boards of affiliated companies. One reason for this strict separation be-tween legal department and management is the English solicitor/barrister situation. Solicitors do not appear in court but instruct barristers. Therefore, there is a natural distance between the solicitor (whether he is in permanent employment or not) and the barrister.

In Germany Rechtsanwälte in permanent employment are not permitted to represent their employer in court. They are expected to be independent if they appear as 'Organ der Rechtspflege' before the court. It is assumed that this independence can not be maintained if the employed Rechtsanwalt appears before a court on behalf of his own company.

In the United States of America more and more company lawyers represent their own company in court because they find it difficult to instruct outside lawyers in complicated matters, in which they as house counsel have more

24. John D. Donnell, op. cit., p. 76.
25. John D. Donnell, op. cit., pp. 79 and 80.

expertise. While many company lawyers do not want to become party to business decisions others have a different opinion and the legal system, in which the company lawyer is educated and working has strong influence on this attitude.

A company lawyer should not get himself pushed into responsibility for business decisions which he is not entitled to make. On the other hand he should not avoid to share the responsibility with his client for decisions which include a combination of commercial and legal questions. A good cooperation between the businessman and the company lawyer should be aimed for: manager and professional give their best talent to solve problems or make decisions which are in the interest of the company and, therefore, in the interest of both of them. This joint activity in a cooperative and collegial spirit will enable the businessman to make the right decision and at the same time give the company lawyer the opportunity to have his legal opinion as well as his business opinion included in the decision-making process. A cooperation of this kind and the joint involvement in the decision-making process require a clear understanding of each other's position.

Managerial skill and legal training do not exclude each other; on the contrary, the legal training can be a very valuable asset for any manager. Today a large number of jurists hold positions of great executive responsibility in the business community, such as banking and insurance, where most of the top managers are lawyers by profession. As early as 1950 Carrol M. Shanks described two qualities of the lawyer which make him especially suitable for management positions: The lawyer is trained to think about and visualize all the various steps necessary to put a particular program into operation; and secondly, somebody with law training and experience 'probably has had more occasion than most laymen to exercise clarity of thought, to reason from the facts, to draw sound conclusions, and then to act'.[26]

The lawyer has to work with many people under varying circumstances. Thus, he learns how to get along with people and how to recognize people of competence. The burden and time involved in the preparation and practice of the law develop patience, and wide reading and intellectual activity tend to develop vision. A natural result of the lawyer's experience through the years is the ability to organize and direct the work of others. All this develops high character and a sense of responsibility.[27]

Melvin Anshen states in his article 'Businessmen, Lawyers and Economists' in Havard Business Review[28] that 'the lawyer is an old associate of the

26. Carroll M. Shanks: 'The Lawyer in Business − His Opportunities and Contributions', 4 Records of the Association of the Bar of the City of New York, 1950, pp. 50-61. W. David Gibson describes in his article 'Business of more Lawyers is Business' (Chemical Week, July 26, 1978, pp. 34-35) the careers of some lawyer-managers in the USA. But also in Europe a number of large companies have former lawyers as top managers.

27. Churchill Rodgers: 'The Lawyer as Life Company Executive', 24 Tennessee Law Review (Summer 1957), pp. 1124-1136.

28. Melvin Anshen: 'Businessmen, Lawyers and Economists How can they reconcile their differences and work together?' 35 Harvard Business Review, March-April 1957, pp. 107-114.

businessman', but until recently lawyers did not make policy decisions or participate in their formulation. The lawyer's role is changing and he is now included in the process to recommend policy objectives and ways to achieve them. This transition is necessary in an economy which is increasingly subjected to public regulation and administration. Governmental influence makes it necessary for management to include lawyers in decisionmaking processes, and management should also be wise enough to accept economic statements which lawyers make. The fact that they have a legal training or working experience does not exclude them from making valuable contributions to economic decisions.

The company law department is a staff function and, as such, is in the same position as market research, personnel, research and development and other staff departments. A modern enterprise can no longer be managed without the organizational principle of staff and line units. Staff units can either be part of the company hierarchy or, as in some companies, stand outside the normal hierarchical structure. While line functions have the authority to make decisions, staff functions normally do not decide themselves but they prepare the decisions, and advise and inform the other management units of the company. Undoubtedly, the technical, economic and legal relations are increasingly complex. The increasing intrusion of governments into business has resulted in a company's inability to make a move without encountering a government regulation. This situation requires a legal opinion and often the judgement of a specialist. The future of the company can, therefore, very well depend on the smooth cooperation between the staff unit legal department and top management which has to make the decisions.

Therefore, line and staff have to supplement each other. Staff managers are not 'second class managers'.[29] Without the thorough and competent preparation of decisions by the staff unit, its advise and information, no vital decision can be made. The members of the company law departments should realize this and not nourish an inferiority complex. They are the guardians and promotors of legality in the decisions of the company, and this is most important for the development of the company.[30]

It is only natural that the integration of the law department in a large company brings about problems because the legal work is different from the managing activity. It is, therefore, important to find ways and methods for close cooperation and the integration of the legal work in the general managerial process of the company.

A company law department can work effectively only if it is supported by the confidence of the company management. In order to establish this confidence, both sides have to understand the tasks which each one has and they have to observe the boundaries of these tasks. Each party must recognize that working closely together will bring the best results for the company. Manage-

29. Reinhard Höhn: 'Die "Stabsoffiziere" dürfen keine Manager zweiter Klasse sein.' Handelsblatt, Mai 30, 1978, p. 19.
30. J. Le Brun: 'Rèflexions sur le Role du Juriste' Le Juriste d'Entreprise, pp. 261-265.

ment personnel who try to dominate the legal department cannot expect unbiased advice and a legal department trying to educate management on non-legal matters cannot expect to be heard in decisions. Between both groups there should be a relationship of respect and confidence.

There exists a special relationship between top management and the legal department: A relationship which normally does not exist with other staff or line departments of the company. The more intensive this relationship is the better it will be for the interest of the company. Top management cannot afford to look upon the legal department as a group of specialists, and company lawyers cannot look upon top management with the distance which sometimes exists in the relationship between client and outside counsel.

The legal department requires full information so that its advice can be based on the complete unbiased knowledge of the subject to be dealt with. Only the full disclosure of the relevant information enables the company lawyer to give to management a complete legal opinion.

To be fully informed about the facts of a case makes it necessary for the company lawyer to be involved in negotiations as early as possible. Many businessmen do not like legal conflicts which disturb the good relationship with customers, suppliers or competitors for long periods of time.[31] But legal conflicts which mostly result from different interpretations of verbal agreements or other misunderstandings can be reduced if the company lawyer participates at the very early stage of business transactions. A prudent manager will be grateful for practical legal advice and will appreciate the assistance of a lawyer.[32]

If the company lawyer's advice makes it possible for the manager to achieve good results, he will be considered not only as a competent lawyer but as a good friend as well. The good relationship with individuals will make it possible to study the problems thoroughly at their earliest stages and at a time when a constructive solution is possible. This will establish a sense of confidence in the lawyer's judgement and integrity. And it often results in a sound leadership position in non-legal cases.[33] Sometimes the house counsel is called upon to serve as a type of house philosopher. The present-day company stands in the center of the democratic process, a continuing series of rising pressures and inevitable responses. Between these stands the company counsel. He has to forestall pressures and to foresee responses that could be damaging for the company. And yet, he cannot be partisan nor believer in the words 'right or wrong my company'. This partiality would not further the interests of the company.[34]

31. F. Verhulst: 'Le Juriste dans L'Industrie', Le Juriste d'Entreprise, pp. 243-252.
32. J.R. Creighton: 'Comment Utiliser plus Efficacement le Conseil Juridique ou le Service Juridique de L'Entreprise' – Le Juriste d'Entreprise, pp. 229-241.
33. Charles S. Maddock: 'The Challenge to House Counsel', Le Juriste d'Entreprise, pp. 345-360.
34. William T. Gosset: 'The Role of the Corporation Counsel' – Washington and Lee Law Review 1956, pp. 129-144.

C. The Company Lawyer as Keeper of the Corporate Conscience?

Companies operate today in a rapidly changing more complex society with often conflicting demands. They have to be good corporate citizens with respect to their employees, customers, suppliers, and the community at large. Summarily, these obligations are sometimes called 'Corporate Conscience'. It has often been stated that the company lawyer is the keeper of the corporate conscience and that he has to warn his company and its management if laws are not observed or standards of commercial morality are infringed upon. This role can be performed by company lawyers because of their professional position, background and freedom. They have staff rather than line functions and, therefore, they are not subject to the permanent strain of reaching turnover figures or production targets. Their success does not depend on such results but upon being men of good judgement. This judgement must include a sound knowledge of law. This gives them a position in which they cannot exercise power over corporate action, but because of their competence are listened to. Here lies the basis of their influence.[35] 'Like the Abbot in the ancient monastery, the clerk to the feudal baron or the chancellor to the king, the corporation counsel is in a position to wield a unique influence'.[36] The professional independence of the company lawyer does not permit him to subordinate his professional judgement to commercial considerations, but his interest in commercial considerations must be part of his professional judgement. He must comprehend the necessities of the business his company is working for. The position and status of the company lawyer give him the opportunity, the right and the duty to advise and encourage, as Hickman calls it 'good corporate citizenship'. This is especially important in a time when the abuse of economic power will almost certainly be followed by governmental restrictions on the company's freedom of action. The company lawyer should be in favour of advising his company to go beyond legal minima. Doing so the company will build up a reservoir of public goodwill.

The behaviour of top management towards the law department and the general counsel is a very important factor in determining the influence of lawyers in a business enterprise. If the chief executive, the managing director, or whatever title might be appropriate in the country concerned, gives weight to the lawyer's legal opinions, this respect will be reflected by management personnel at lower levels of the organization. Without such respect for and attention to the legal opinion of the general counsel, the company law departments' effectiveness and satisfaction will tend to be reduced.[37]

Management is responsible to the share-holders for the conduct of the company. The general counsel has to make sure that all laws and regulations

---

35. H. Thomas Austern: 'Corporate Counsel Communication: Is Anybody Listening?', The Business Lawyer, July 1962, pp. 868-876.
36. Leon E. Hickman: 'The Emerging Role of the Corporate Counsel', The Business Lawyer, April 1957, pp. 216-228.
37. John D. Donnell, op. cit., p. 176.

are observed, not only by the company but also by its personnel. In order to enable him to fulfil this function he must have the full support and backing of the top management of the company. Therefore, there exists a joint responsibility of chief executive officer and general counsel for the observation of rules and regulations. This joint responsibility has been described very well in a directive issued by the chief executive officer of a large American company to his general counsel which reads as follows:

'Special Responsibility of Certain Officers to the Board of Directors.
The General Counsel, Chief Staff Officer and Director of Auditing have a special responsibility to the Board of Directors. The nature of that responsibility and the process for carrying it out are described in two letters sent to each of them.
Following is the text of the letters to the General Counsel from the President and from the Chairman to the Board:

From the President:

As President and chief executive officer, I have an obligation to the Board to see that they get all the information they need in order to perform their function effectively. In order to give the Board maximum assurance that there will be no important gaps in the information they receive. I wish to charge certain selected officers with the responsibility of initiating reports to the Board on their own behalf under certain circumstances.
As General Counsel, you are one of those officers. If, as the Corporation's chief legal officer, you either
1. disagree with my decisions to overrule a professional opinion of yours on a matter where you consider the impact to be important to the welfare of the organization,
   and
2. on which I have chosen not to report to the directors that such difference of view exists,
   or
3. feel that a piece of information I have chosen not to give to the Board is material and should be given to them,
it shall be your responsibility to bring the matter promptly to the attention of the Board and make your views known. In either instance, I instruct you to talk to me first, so that we can determine whether it is simply a case of misunderstanding between us which we can deal with as such. If that is not the case and you do not persuade me to change my position, you will then make your report on the matter to the Chairman of the Board or, in his absence, to the Chairman of the Audit Committee. I desire to accompany you to make my own views known at the same time. You must not, however, allow such desire on my part to keep

you from making your report with or without me.

While I have described this instruction to you as springing from my obligation to the Board, I also see it as serving me well in another way; by ensuring that I have the support of our chief legal officer in a given important decision unless you have promptly made it clear that I do not.

From the Chairman of the Board:

You have received from the President instruction regarding your obligation under certain circumstances to report to the Board on your own initiative. He has instructed you to report to me or to the Chairman of the Audit Committee.

This is to inform you that, if you bring such an issue to me and I find that I do not share your view of it, I will, nevertheless, arrange an audience for you with the full Board if you so request. Having been given that facility, you have the responsibility to use it if, in your judgement, it is in the best interest of the Corporation for you to do so.'

This instruction to the general counsel in a strictly hierarchically organized business enterprise of considerable size is self-explanatory. It results partly from the difficulties in which many boards of directors found themselves in the United States of America in the last years. But, it also shows the responsibility which president and chairman have to the board of directors as representatives of the shareholders and as representatives of the public which has an interest to see that the business of the company is conducted in a legal way. The letters express a deep understanding for the necessity of having the general counsel and thus the company law department involved in the well-being of the company. They also show the responsibility which rests upon the legal officers of the company probably more than on most other management positions, even though they are not responsible for the financial and economic status of the company. The letters also show the necessity for an intense and close cooperation between top management personnel and company lawyers. Other companies have institutionalized safeguards within the corporation to assist the lawyer in handling corporate misconduct if it should be discovered. For example, the Bylaws of General Motors Corporation provide that the general counsel is a corporate officer who can be appointed and removed only by the Board of Directors. This also gives the chief legal officer a more direct relationship to the board itself and enables the general counsel to point out weak situations in the company. The underlying idea is to make the general counsel as independent as possible and thus enable him to give impartial advice and recommendations to the Board of Directors as the ultimate responsible institution of the company.[38]

The position of the company lawyer in relation to ethical problems is very

38. The Ethical Responsibilities of Lawyers were discussed extensively at a Panel, Ethical Responsibilities of Corporate Lawyers, The Business Lawyer, Special Issue, March 1978.

sensitive and very difficult. The general counsel is a member of the company team and not the umpire. Depending on his professional status and relationship with his colleagues he can be very effective in maintaining the integrity and high ethical standards of his company.[39] The American Bar Association Code of Professional Responsibility, Ethical Consideration 5-18 states:

> 'A lawyer employed or retained by a corporation . . . owes his allegiance to the entity and not to a stockholder, director, officer . . . or other person connected with the entity.'

Because of the responsibility to the corporate entity, as distinguished from the lawyer's responsibility to management, the company lawyer should advise his company and its management not only on legal questions, but he should be an adviser in the broadest sense of the word. This includes the right of the company lawyer to advise on ethical and moral issues.[40] The concept of Dean Redlich for the role of the legal adviser is to do everything possible to make certain that the client acts:

1. legally;
2. morally;
3. wisely.

The problem can best be summarized as follows:

> 'The lawyer should be expected to maintain a high moral and ethical standard of conduct, and it is degrading to our profession for lawyer to refuse to advise against improper conduct merely because it is not legal and he has, in effect, been told to mind his own business'.[41]

Great difficulties can be foreseen if the company lawyer is regarded and expected to play the dual role of adviser and policeman. In order to be an effective adviser he needs the confidence of his clients, i.e. his management colleagues. This is, of course, not compatible with policing activities. Top management has to make the clear and unmistaken statement that it expects all members of the company to conduct themselves lawfully. This message has to be transmitted by the higher levels of management to the lower levels. But just preaching this gospel is not sufficient. Top management has to live up to these statements itself even if the observance of such principles means in effect a reduction of the company's profits.[42]

---

39. Mendes Hershman: 'Special Problems of Inside Counsel for Financial Institutions', The Business Lawyer, Special Issue, March 1978, pp. 1435-1448.
40. Dean Norman Redlich: 'Should a Lawyer cross the Murky Divide?', The Business Lawyer, November 1975, pp. 478-481.
41. Dean Norman Redlich, op. cit., p. 481.
42. E.L. Hollis: 'What I expect from a Corporate Client', The Business Lawyer, April 1966, pp. 842-847.

II. Functions of the Company Law Department

A paper prepared for Law School students by the Committee on Corporate Law Departments, Section of Corporation, Banking and Business Law of the American Bar Association states:

'The broad general function of the law department is to delineate legal boundaries within which the management of the corporation is free to exercise its ingenuity in successfully managing the corporate enterprise. Its function is not to cover up or conceal illegal activities. It is the responsibility of corporate lawyers, however, to attempt to find ways legally to achieve proper corporate objectives'.[1]

The same paper continues to say that all the company officers and other management employees and the lawyers themselves have to understand that the company policy is to comply with the law as the company law department construes it.

This does not, of course, mean that the law department runs the business. It does mean that the executives secure their interpretation of the law from the law department and make their decision in light of such interpretation. The executives may, of course, assume business risks involved in certain courses of action. A company law department has to administer the company's legal activities in such a way as to ensure

1. maximum protection of the legal rights of the company consistent with the performance of the company's other responsibilities
   and
2. proper discharge of the company's legal obligations.[2]

William T. Gossett, at that time General Counsel of Ford Motor Company, points out in a lecture 'The Role of the Corporate Counsel' the importance of the activity which the company lawyer has in judging his company's actions before they are undertaken. This includes constant observation and appraisal of the progress of free society in which his company exists.[3] Orville F. Grahame, Vice-President and General Counsel of The Massachusetts Protec-

1. Law Practice in a Corporate Law Department, reproduced by Permission of the American Bar Association, 1971.
2. Austin Gavin: 'The Educational Function of the Corporate Legal Department', The Business Lawyer, January 1961, pp. 370-376.
3. William T. Gosset: 'The Role of the Corporation Counsel', Washington and Lee Law Review, vol. XIII, 1956, no. 2, pp. 129-144.

tive Companies lists the services of the company law department.[4] Other publications list the responsibilities of the company law department.[5, 6] In the 1950s and 1960s a number of publications described the functions which the company law department has in its business organization. Nowadays it is no longer necessary to list the various activities of company lawyers because they have become an integral part of the business organization and they discharge all legal matters of the company, including many administrative problems. Therefore their role no longer requires definitions or lists. They are of the same importance as other service departments of a large company. The National Industrial Conference Board (1965) studied 'Top Management Organization in Divisionalized Companies' as part of its 'Studies in Personnel Policy'. On page 63 of this study 'The Legal-Secretarial Function' is described. The study included 76 companies and therefore can be considered to be representative.

One reply of a company defined the legal function as follows:

'The unit ensures that the company's objectives, policies, programs and indeed whatever the company or its agents do, are in consonance with existing legislation. Such description suggests that the legal staff might be at the heart of a vast legal control apparatus. This is not usually the case. In fact, companies have been criticized for having too few control procedures in legal matters.'

Another company stated:

'The large majority of large corporate legal staffs supply legal services to the entire company, corporate staff, divisions and units. The emphasis of services is characteristic of the function'.

In some companies a combined legal-secretarial unit exists. The executive in charge of this unit is at the same time the general counsel and the secretary of the company.

According to the study typical responsibilities of the secretary are:

- 'The secretary provides certain services to and for the board. He prepares and keeps the records of the board of directors and its committees. He conducts the correspondence of the board, issueing among other things all calls for meetings of the board, its committees, and all stockholders' meetings.
- A second major activity involves the company's stock certificates and other corporate documents.
- A third area in which the secretary has responsibility is stockholder relations. He is responsible for printing and distributing the annual report and

4. Orville F. Grahame: 'What I expected of the Corporate Law Department?', 49 American Bar Association Journal, February 1963, pp. 159-161.
5. Andrew Hendrix Knight: 'The Handling of Legal Matters of Corporations by its own Law Department', 12 Alabama Law Review 119, (Fall 1959).
6. Charles S. Maddock: 'The Corporation Law Department', 30 Harvard Business Review, 119, March/April 1952.

for handling correspondence between the company management and stockholders'.[7]

This list of secretarial responsibilities in Anglo-Saxon companies shows that the secretary is responsible for legal matters which in continental European companies are defined as part of the company law and therefore are part of the activity of the company legal department. It is only reasonable that in many American and also British companies the secretary is at the same time also the chief lawyer of the company.

In the article 'Board Chairman, Presidents, Legal Counsel: Some Aspects of their Jobs', which was published in The Conference Board Record of January 1967,[8] is stated that in one fifth of the companies included in the survey, the house counsel (general counsel) was a member of the board of directors. In an additional third of these companies the house counsel attended all board meetings even though he was not a board member. The reason for this was to give immediate advice to aid in the board's deliberations and expedite its decisions. The president of a metal working machinery company explained it like this: 'In view of today's legal complications, we find it both desirable and necessary that our legal counsel serve on the board of directors'.[9] Some companies replied that according to their opinions the legal counsel cannot be effective unless he learns first hand of the business taken up at board meetings. Other considerations cited for inviting counsel to serve on the board are respect for the counsel's business judgement, and in the case of outside counsel, the experience which he has acquired as a director of other corporations.

Also in most European companies the chief legal adviser attends the meetings of the board of directors or supervisory boards, even if he is not a member. He is responsible for drawing the minutes of the proceedings and has to give legal advice. This tendency became more important since members of the work force serve in supervisory councils under the legislation existing in a number of European countries, especially in the Federal Republic of Germany. Here the company attorney has to reply to legal problems coming up in board meetings. Members of the board representing the shareholders do not always have the detailed legal expertise to solve differences of opinion with employee representatives or trade union representatives as members of the board or to construe the relevant legislation.

It should not be forgotten that 'the executives of a corporation must try to earn profits for the stockholders while obeying legislative commands and prohibitions couched in language that is at best vague and in some cases downright incomprehensible to everyone except the judges of courts of review'.[10]

7. The National Industrial Conference Board, op. cit., p. 64.
8. The Conference Board Record, 'Board Chairman, Presidents, Legal Counsel: Some Aspects of their Jobs', January 1967, pp. 9-12.
9. The Conference Board Record, op. cit., p. 11.
10. Walker B. Davis: 'Reflections of a Kept Lawyer', 53 American Bar Association Journal, 1967, pp. 349, 350.

Therefore, the most important and probably also most valuable part of the services rendered by the company law department is the practising of preventive law. 'Preventive or prophylactic law avoids the legal complications before they happen so that they never have to be dealt with. Thus it can be said that the corporation needs a legal department to reduce the need for a lawyer'.[11] Members of management expect of the company legal department that it practises preventive law so that the activities of the company will avoid legal situations which could result in litigation or difficulties at some later date.[12] This can only be achieved if the manager seeks the advice of the company lawyer during the formative considerations of policy and practices of his company.

The company legal department has three advantages for the manager:
1. His immediate availability,
2. his knowledge of corporate policy, personnel and business background and
3. his ability to practise preventive law by being in on the ground floor of company planning where he can point out legal problems throughout the company without waiting to have such matters referred to him.[13]

Therefore, it is most important to educate managers so that they consult the law department beforehand and not afterwards. It is beneficial for a lawyer in the legal department to have a good relationship with the rest of the management of the company so that full use can be made of the services of the legal department.

The company lawyer is close to management. He knows the business of his company and he is consulted on a regular basis and thus will be able both to assist the business as far as laws and regulations are concerned and to promote clarity of ideas and expression within the company. During the last twenty years the company law department has developed from its function as on the spot adviser to a full fledge legal staff which is capable of solving almost all legal problems of the company.[14]

The relationship between company lawyers and business executives can be improved if the company lawyer observes in his work and advice certain principles which will further the businessman's confidence in the usefulness of the lawyer's assistance. In a lecture before the First Annual Institute on Corporate Counsel of Fordham University School of Law, New York, N.Y., on April 2, 1959, George E. Diethelm, Vice-President and General Counsel of the American Sugar Refining Company, mentioned four major rules for reaching this objective:

11. Austin Gavin, op. cit., pp. 370-376.
12. Sylvester C. Smith jr.: 'The Business Executive, Corporate Counsel and General Practitioner', The Business Lawyer, January 1958, pp. 220-229.
13. Leon E. Hickman: 'The Need and Utilization of Retained Counsel', Proceedings of Wisconsins Fifth Annual House Counsel Institute, 68, 1969.
14. David S. Ruder: 'A Suggestion for Increased Use of Corporate Law Department in Modern Corporations', The Business Lawyer, January 1968, pp. 341-363.

'The advice must be timely; the matters discussed must be confidential; the time of the executive must not be wasted by unnecessarily long conferences or memoranda; and the lawyer must not appropriate a credit for any business decision that is made'.[15]

Management and other employees should recognize that it is desirable to consult the law department at the beginning of a project and not after decisions have already been made.

Education is an essential function of all legal departments. Gavin divides the educational function into two categories:

a. Reporting of current legal developments,
b. Other background educational activities.

A. Reporting of Current Legal Developments

Report on legislation or bills, court decisions and other reports of legal relevance can be of utmost importance for the company. The extent to which a legal department monitors and reports on legislative activities depends of course on the size of the company and the department, the nature of its business and the way in which it may be effected by legislation of this kind. Especially in countries where legal departments have either themselves or through business associations close contacts with governmental agencies which draft new proposed legislation, it is very important to use such contacts. Often the officials charged with drafting legislation are grateful for information from practitioners because frequently legislative projects are very theoretical due to lack of information. Here the company lawyer can practise a certain influence on proposed legislation by explaining beforehand to government and parliament the effects and possible shortcomings of the project. 'The company lawyer must not only be aware of possible developments, but he must also take an interest in legislative matters. The legal department may bring to the attention of legislators the effects of proposed legislation. It may even assist in drafting such legislation'.[16]

Reports on legislation or judicial decisions can influence planning and future activities of the company. Therefore, it is necessary to bring these developments to the attention of the executives involved. Some legal departments have worked out procedures for written reports on such developments and these written reports are widely distributed throughout the company. Other legal departments make annual or quarterly reports to management. Such reports on the activity of the legal department include a section on developments in legislation and court decisions. The advantage of such reports is that the legal department surveys its own activity for a certain reporting period. It thus has the opportunity to present to management many activities which probably otherwise would not come to the attention of management.

15. Austin Gavin, op. cit., p. 371.
16. Charles S. Maddock, op. cit., pp. 119, 127.

In such reports trends can be pointed out and various separate developments can be related in the context of their effect on the company. Tendencies can be shown especially if the claims department or insurance matters are included in such reports. For management these reports are an excellent opportunity to learn about the activities of the legal department and the legal pitfalls of the company which become obvious from such reports. Of course, the operating departments should avoid considering the report as an instrument for divulging their faults. But the accumulation of cases concerning the activity of an operating unit can show that the management of this unit is not acting with the legal precaution that must be demanded of all operating units in a large company.

Within the legal department the general counsel should educate his lawyers to collect material for such reports, and to invest time and effort to make the reports attractive for management to read. He should himself give the report the final polish and if possible decide beforehand about special points of interest to be explained more fully in the reporting period. Thus the emphasis can be shifted from one activity of the legal department to the other and over a certain period of time a complete picture of the importance of the work done in the department is given.

B. Other Background Educational Activities

The most valuable educational work is done by the members of a legal department during their day-to-day consultation with members of the other departments in the company. They are in permanent communication with the non-legal executives of the company who are their colleagues in the company though they are not colleagues in the same profession.

The lawyer of the legal department knows the business and the plans of the company, he is part of the company and involved with it every day. Therefore, the operating executive does not avoid discussions with inhouse counsel. He is grateful for being alerted to potential legal risks, particularly if this is accompanied by suggested alternate methods of solving business problems. Free and open discussions are possible and usual between the executive personnel and inside counsel. The familiarity of inside counsel with all branches of the company and its problems can be of great help to the executive manager who sometimes sees only his own division and therefore his own problems. In other words inside counsel can have a kind of amalgamating effect between the divisions and units of the company and he can thus be of a very positive influence far beyond his professional job.[17] In this permanent contact the company lawyer can be very concrete and practical. The house counsel would commit suicide if he would lock himself in an ivory tower.[18]

17. Walter Kolvenbach: 'Organization of Legal Departments in Larger Corporations with Special Consideration of Inside/Outside Counsel', International Legal Practitioner, May 1977, pp. 10-19.
18. Maurice-André Flamme: 'Le Role et les Fonctions du Juriste d'Entreprise', Le Juriste d'Entreprise, p. 41.

A close working relationship can be established with other departments of the company and the closer the cooperation, the more frequent and productive the opportunities for educational activities will be. Informal discussions establish confidence between the business executive and his colleague in the company law department and he will often go with his problems to the law department in a very informal way depending on the closeness of the personal relationship developed in the course of working together. This will induce the manager to come to the lawyer as early as possible to solicit the assistance and the support of the company law department for his projects. It would be ideal if every manager were a combination of businessman and lawyer. Identifying the legal implications of specific decisions is not easy. Therefore, management must create systems that will automatically bring questions which could have legal implications to the attention of the company legal department. The training that the lawyer has received permits him to identify legal problems more readily than laymen. If a manager fails to identify a problem or does not call on the company lawyers after a problem has been detected, the company can suffer serious damage.[19]

If a legal department exists for many years and has established such contacts, the educational activities of the past will be very useful for the company. Without confidence and understanding there will not be a good working climate between company lawyers and management personnel. The result of such lack of cooperation can easily be, as one commentator describes rather unkindly: 'The house counsel is still, usually, the only man in the lot, who can read and write — as any lawyer who has had to go over corporate records kept without benefit of counsel knows to his dismay and sometimes to his sorrow'.[20]

The attitude expressed in these words explains why in many countries, among them Germany, jurists are not very well liked by their surroundings.[21] This attitude is also expressed in a well-known joke: Discussing, which profession is the oldest on earth, the doctor states that his profession is the oldest because it accomplished the job with Adam and his rib. The architect points out that even before this event, some architect must have created the world out of the then existing chaos. And the lawyer asks the obvious question: 'And who created the chaos?' . . .

It is needless to say that the spirit of confidence and the preparedness to cooperate cannot be reached through regulations or orders: General Foods Corporation had a manual prepared for those who might use the law departments' services and this manual expressed the rather strong warning: 'He who

19. Lawrence E. Hicks: 'The Manager and the Law: Using Legal Counsel', Manager's Forum, May 1975.
20. Adolf A. Baerle jr.: 'The Changing Role of the Corporation and its Counsel', Record of the Association of the Bar of the City of New York, 1955, pp. 266-278.
21. Wilhelm Wengler: 'Über die Unbeliebtheit der Juristen', Neue Juristische Wochenschrift 1959, pp. 1705-1708.

is his own lawyer has a fool for a client'.[22] This statement is certainly too strong and aggressive. It shows, however, that the necessity for legal assistance in the day-to-day business must be recognized.

Also the organization of the legal department can support the educational activity. If one or more lawyers are assigned to each major department or unit and follow closely the day-to-day activities of that department this contact will result in an intense working relationship.

Having established confidence, cooperation and close relationship the practising of preventive law can begin. The company lawyer has the most effective means to practise preventive law and to be involved before crucial events occur. It depends upon his personal relationship with his counterparts in management whether he is involved in certain business transactions before legally binding steps are taken or before, for instance, advertising material is released to the public. Also in this field, preventive law is most important: the company lawyer can check, control and cooperate in the drafting of advertisements and, thereby, avoid unfavourable reactions by consumer protection organizations or competitors for violation of unfair competition legislation or similar rules which exist in most countries.

Professional craftsmanship of the highest order is required of corporate lawyers. They are in a position to see the overall corporate picture; and because they are consulted in advance of decisions, they are part of the team participating in the decisionmaking process. The performance of preventive law practice is by its nature creative and vital to the corporation.[23]

Our business world is developing towards a new social-economic system. This system is marked by more rules and regulations (in Europe also) and Europe, therefore, is marching along the same road which the United States of America have marched some twenty years ago and are still marching! The numerous regulations of the Common Market and mountains of legislation in each member state have forced managers to be more professional and it has forced the company lawyer to cooperate more closely with the other specialists in the company. As in the technical field, specialization for lawyers has become inevitable. The lawyer who is only a generalist or coordinator has to become either a specialist himself or he has to call on the specialized lawyer more and more.[24] Frequently the specialist to be used in a case or problem will be an outside counsel who has sometimes more experience in special fields of law than the company lawyer can have.[25]

22. National Industrial Conference Board, Studies in Business Policy, no. 39, 'Corporate Legal Departments', 17, 1950.
23. Law Practice in a Corporate Law Department, op. cit., p. 4.
24. J.M. Deleuze: 'La Prise de Décision et L'Evolution du Role du Juriste d'Entreprise', Bulletin de l'Association Belge des Juristes d'Entreprise, no. 6, 1970, pp. 56-63.
25. Jean de Lanauze, 'De la Bonne Utilisation des Conseils par leur Client', Cahiers de droit de L'entreprise, No. 3, 1976.

III. House Counsel versus Outside Counsel?

A. The Advantage of Using Outside Counsel

It is often mentioned that some rivalry does exist between lawyers in general practice and house counsel.[1] Theoretically the existence of the company legal department could make the employment of outside counsel unnecessary. But this theory has not been proved correct, because even in companies with a large, highly developed and specialized legal department there is still a wide field of activity for outside counsel. Even a well staffed and well-organized law department cannot supply all the legal services required by a large company and its affiliates. Therefore company lawyers are making increasingly more effective use of outside counsel. It should not be overlooked that there are discussions on this subject, especially in countries where jurists, working in company legal departments as employees of the company, are admitted to the bar, as in the USA, the United Kingdom and the Federal Republic of Germany. But also in countries where jurists with a permanent employee-relationship to their company cannot be admitted to the bar, the attorneys at law sometimes tend to look at the members of legal departments as competitors who take away prospective work from them. It is not necessary to mention that this is not the case and that this opinion prevails with practitioners who do not work regularly with company legal departments. Outside law firms are frequently used and have proved most useful to industry. Instead of rivalry, which fortunately is disappearing a natural division of labour has developed — work of one nature is handled almost exclusively by house counsel and work af another nature is turned over almost exclusively to the law firms.[2]

A survey published by the National Conference Board in October 1959[3] showed that most of the companies involved in this survey retained outside counsel even if they had internal legal departments. Of course the frequency differed. Outside counsel was retained least frequently by the largest compa-

---

1. Stephen E. Davis: 'Corporate Law Departments — A New Look at the "New Look"', The Business Lawyer January 1963, pp. 659-671.
2. Stephen E. Davis: 'House Counsel: The Lawyer with a single client', American Bar Association Journal September 1955, pp. 830-832.
3. National Conference Board: 'Business Record, Organization for Legal Work', October 1959, pp. 463-468.

nies participating in the survey because 'the volume of legal work is large enough to warrant having on our staff lawyers who are specialists or have become thoroughly versed in particular types of problems'.[4] Most companies who retain outside counsel mentioned that they deal with matters pertaining to certain fields of law where the advice of specialists is called for, court room work, and certain areas where ethical considerations prohibit the use of inside attorneys. A survey conducted by the Conference Board ten years later supported the result of the first survey.[5] It is interesting to note the advantages of using outside counsel as they were stated in this survey. The benefit mentioned most often by the participating firms is the expertise and experience of outside counsel. Numbering the advantages according to the replies received, most companies declared that they are using outside counsel because it is generally less expensive, especially for smaller firms. The second argument is the broad range of experience and up-to-date expertise available in outside law firms.

Other advantages of outside counsel are that they may be less partisan than a house counsel who knows intimately the men with whom he is dealing and the importance which a legal opinion might have for some decisions in, for instance, marketing questions. Total immersion in the organization can place a strain on inside counsel's independent judgement. This can result in wishful thinking in favour of the company. Considering the importance and consequences of certain decisions, the legal responsibility can be very heavy. The use of an outside counsel for such critical questions adds experienced independent guidance to the legal opinion developed by the company's own legal department and thus strengthens the factual basis for decision-making.

B. Relationship between House Counsel and Outside Counsel

In cases where outside counsel is retained the relationship between inside counsel and his outside counterparts is most important. It has been stated that outside counsel today can, in many cases, solve company problems more effectively than at the times when there were no legal departments in large companies.[6] The reason for this is that many business executives are not fully aware of the legal implications of their activities. Even if they are aware, they are often reluctant to call upon the help of outside counsel because to many people consultation with a lawyer implies delay and expenses; moreover, it might result in a negative recommendation.

In addition, it is difficult for non-professional company officials to determine

4. National Conference Board, op. cit., p. 464.
5. 'Legal Organization in the Manufacturing Corporation', The Conference Board Record, August 1969, pp. 42-47.
6. George M. Szabad and Daniel Gersel: 'Inside vs. Outside Counsel', The Business Lawyer November 1972, pp. 235-251.

how far the outside lawyer should participate, and the lawyer himself may be reluctant to suggest a larger participation in decision-making processes because the company might get the impression that he wants to acquire work for himself. I would like to quote the words which one author on the subject uses:

'...the outside lawyer working within a corporate structure, without the benefit of inside corporate lawyers, always faces the difficulty that everybody's guards will be up lest something be discovered that would reflect adversely upon one of the corporate individuals involved. An outside lawyer simply cannot move freely within a corporate structure any more than an alien substance can be tolerated by the human body.

The interposition of a corporate legal department has made all the difference in the world in this relationship. Corporate counsels are insiders, part of the corporate team, and it is accepted appropriate that they know where the bodies are buried. They employ the outside counsel as their advisers and colleagues. The corporate counsel makes the inside investigation. They deal with outside counsel as professionals of equal rank. They are professionally qualified to diagnose the points of legal sensitivity and the outside lawyer can test the analysis freely in a discussion among professionals of equal status'.[7]

It is hard to describe in better words the relationship between these two parts of the legal profession. House counsel has access to all internal documents which might be of importance in a case. For the outside counsel it would be difficult to participate in lengthy internal discussions or even more in internal decision-making processes. This is impossible not only from an organizational and practical point of view, but the outside counsel would have to spend most or all of his time in the company and thus gradually become a company law department member himself, though under a different name...

The company lawyer has become a specialist in the legal problems, the personalities and the business of his company. This knowledge develops by daily association with company personnel, constant participation in conferences out of which company policy is developed, and a knowledge of company matters possible only through daily participation in their making. An outside lawyer could hardly expect to reach this skill. In general practice the development goes in a different direction. Law firms represent many clients and the legal problems emerge from a variety of situations mostly in unrelated industries. The practitioner has to deal with businessmen from different companies, both large and small. He will see a number of contradictory approaches to the same basic problem, and he will develop skills in observing what succeeds and what fails in a given situation.[8] These examples are illustrating that some combination of inside counsel and outside counsel is the nearly universal rule. The responsibility for competent legal guidance of

7. Leon Hickman: 'Corporate Legal Departments re – visited', New York Bar Journal October 1971, pp. 391-393.
8. Leon E. Hickman: 'Corporate Counsel and the Bar', The Business Lawyer July 1959, pp. 925-943.

the company becomes a joint one. A division of work develops which will be advantageous for both sides.[9]

It seems fitting to attempt to define the relationship which ideally should exist between the company legal department and outside counsel so that both can fully benefit by this cooperation. The company lawyer and the outside counsel have to recognize the place which each has and thus strengthen each other's role. The outside counsel must accept the role occupied by the company lawyer. He must understand that when he does legal work for a company his client normally is the member of the legal department who is handling the matter. His direct responsibility is to this company lawyer though, of course, his duty of fidelity also includes the company which is his client. It is only normal that the legal personality 'company' in such cases is represented by a human being and in each case this is the company lawyer.[10]

The company legal department selects the attorney who will do legal work for the company. Criteria for the selection can only be how well he will carry out his task. Personal affinities or connections to the products or to the finances of the company can be very costly. The attorney should be chosen solely on the basis of an evaluation of his worth as the best obtainable expert for the case. Technical talent and competence, as well as political sensitivity, must be expected of a good outside lawyer.[11]

Relations between the company legal department and outside counsel should be molded by the greatest possible degree of mutual confidence and respect. Therefore the company lawyer working on the case should accept the judgement of outside counsel with respect to matters of local law and trial tactics. On the other hand, it is worthwhile to supervise the work of outside counsel closely, especially in view of the legal department's thorough knowledge of facts and policies within the company. Therefore all litigation should be carefully followed. Sometimes even legal research or fact research within the legal department may greatly strengthen the case in the hands of the outside counsel. It has to be binding for the entire personnel of the company that relations with outside lawyers are channeled and handled only through the legal department. This avoids competitive situations between company lawyers and outside counsel, and it prevents non-lawyers in the company from being tempted to build up criticisms for the legal department by encouraging negative comments from outside counsel. There should be a clear company policy that only the legal department and no other company officials will submit work to outside counsel for review. Thus the lawyers in the company can explain to the outside counsel the reason for the position which they have taken and the counsel will receive the necessary facts to make the right

9. Stan C. Kaiman: 'Corporate Legal Services: A Primer', The Business Lawyer April 1971, pp. 1131-1144.
10. Frank L. Seamans: 'Relations between Corporate Legal Departments and Outside Counsel', The Business Lawyer April 1960, pp. 633-637.
11. Lawrence A. Sullivan: 'How to Choose and Use a Lawyer', Harvard Business Review September/October 1957, pp. 61-67.

decision. If there is disagreement between the legal department and outside counsel there will, nevertheless, be a common understanding of the underlying facts. This enables the legal department to place before management the complete view and reports of outside counsel, especially when they differ from the views of the legal department.[12]

C. Advantage of Exclusive Relationship between Legal Department and Outside Counsel

This system of exclusive relationship between the legal department and outside counsel enables the head of the legal department to retain control of the legal expenses of the company for which he is responsible. As a company employee he is best qualified to judge the quality of the outside counsel's work and the reasonableness of his charges. Any charges of outside law firms, therefore, must be approved by the legal department before payment.

There can be another advantage of channeling all contacts with the outside lawyer through the company legal department: the attorney-client privilege. I do not intend to discuss here the legal situations, which differ from country to country. But there are some countries which grant to any attorney, regardless of whether he is employed by a company or not, a privilege that prohibits disclosure of confidential communications between an attorney and his client.[13] This important legal principle which apparently was developed by English courts has been defined as follows:

'Where legal advice of any kind is sought from a professional legal adviser in his capacity as such, the communications relating to that purpose, made in confidence by the client, are at this instance, permanently protected from disclosure by himself or by the legal adviser, except the protection be waived'.[14]

In the US, a court decision stated that the 'type of service performed by house counsel is substantially like that performed by many members of the large urban law firms. The distinction is chiefly that the house counsel gives advice to one regular client, the outside counsel to several regular clients'.[15] Therefore, the American company lawyer has the same attorney privilege as his colleague in private practice. Letters and memoranda exchanged between house counsel and outside counsel are protected from disclosure as privileged, provided that primarily legal matters are dealt with.[16] Numerous cases in the

12. Lawrence S. Asey: 'Organization of a Corporate Legal Department', The Business Lawyer July 1959, pp. 944-956.
13. Richard S. Maurer: 'Privileged Communications and the Corporate Counsel', The Business Lawyer July 1961, pp. 959-983.
14. 'The Lawyer-Client Privilege: Its Application to Corporations, the Role of Ethics, and its Possible Curtailment', Northwestern University Law Review, Vol. 56, 1961, pp. 235-262.
15. David Simon: 'The Attorney-Client Privilege as Applied to Corporations', The Yale Law Journal, 1956, pp. 952-990.
16. Thomas R. Hunt: 'Corporate Law Department Communications – Privilege and Discovery', Vanderbilt Law Review, 1959, pp. 287-309.

US have dealt with the protection of house counsel documents.[17] It is interesting to compare the situation in a divisionalized company, where members of division law departments report to division executives and not to the General Counsel as in centralized law departments.[18] Another problem results from the work of lawyers in departments with mixed legal and business matters.[19] But also for the lawyers in the legal department, internal rules have to be observed to make sure that the privilege is maintained.[20] In view of the often confusing legal situation and the many judgements which courts have made in the various fields of law, it can be concluded that for American legal departments this question is of great importance and that the existence or non-existence of the privilege can have far reaching consequences for the company.[21] The professional privilege of attorneys at law is differently regulated in the various European countries. The national laws of the nine member states of the European Economic Community differ on the question of the extent of immunity of lawyer-client documents from disclosure. Therefore, Community Law will not necessarily be the same as any one national law. The European Commission will have to define its attitude on this subject especially in view of the role which this immunity plays in cartel proceedings. Also in this field of law it must be expected that European Law will differ from some of the laws of the member states and that this European legal concept will apply to 'European cases' only − a rather confusing perspective. All member states have in common a general principle of law under which documents passing between a lawyer and his client have a certain immunity from disclosure in proceedings. This immunity is nowhere absolute. The attitude of the Commission and especially the extent of the immunity under European Law is open. Most important in this connection is the immunity right of salaried lawyers. If consulted in his capacity as legal adviser, he must have the same right as a lawyer in private practice. Communications between companies and their in-house legal departments cannot be demanded for inspection by the Directorates of the Commission. A distinction between the private practitioner and the salaried lawyer regarding immunity from disclosure to the Commission cannot be accepted and would result in total legal confusion. It can only be hoped that the European Court of Justice will ultimately recognize this principle and that this court will not differentiate between two types of lawyers as some commission officials occasionally do.

17. W.M.N. Strack: 'Attorney-Client Privilege − House Counsel', The Business Lawyer April 1957, pp. 229-256.
18. F.W. Dietmar Schaefer: 'The Attorney-Client Privilege in the Modern Business Corporation', The Business Lawyer July 1965, pp. 989-995.
19. James T. Haight: 'Keeping the Privilege Inside the Corporation', The Business Lawyer, January 1963, pp. 551-561.
20. Ralph M. Carson: 'Privilege and the Work-Product Rule in Corporate Law Deparments', The Business Lawyer April 1959, pp. 771-781.
21. James H. Kerr: 'Developments in Corporate Law', The Business Lawyer July 1963, pp. 917-929.

D. Legal Fields which are Typical for Joint Handling between House Counsel and Outside Counsel

1. I would like to describe some typical examples of faithful cooperation between the company lawyer and the outside attorney. All company law departments have special fields of law in which they are more experienced than most outside counsels can be. One example are company lawyers in companies producing branded articles and consumer goods, especially those countries where the legislation and case law on unfair competition are very important. The company lawyer has to make sure that all rules and regulations which deal with branded articles i.e., trademark laws, patent laws, regulations on packaging, contents of packaging, labelling design, etc., are observed. To control this, besides the legal experience a full knowledge of competitive packages and the situation in the market place is required. For outside counsel it would be almost impossible to remember the many packages, slogans or trademarks that are being used by the competitors.

2. If infringements are reported normally contact is made with the company lawyer in the competitive firm and a professional discussion takes place, exploring the opposite opinions and explaining questions which might come up. If this does not result in agreement either an injunction, a law suit or arbitration proceedings are instituted. In all these alternatives the outside attorney is a most important partner. He has special skills in litigation which normally a company lawyer does not have. Most companies do not have enough litigation in any field of law to occupy the major part of the time of one company lawyer. An attorney's work in court is only done well by someone who is there regularly. Therefore all court work should be handled by outside lawyers. The actual conduct and technique of the trial are his sole responsibility. He will be briefed by the company lawyer. The company lawyer will consult all technical experts and marketing experts within the company to enable the outside lawyer to become familiar with the subject and to deepen his knowledge through discussion with and questioning of these experts. The consultations take place, of course, in the presence of the company lawyer who knows the mentality of his colleague in the legal department of the competing firm and who, on the other hand, can provide the outside lawyer with all information he requires.[22] The outside attorney representing the company has the primary responsibility for all documents filed in court. This involves the obligation to prepare drafts of the papers sufficiently far in advance so that the company lawyer can study the drafts and comment on them. The outside attorney furthermore has to report to the company lawyer as the case progresses because management will normally discuss the situation of pending cases with the company lawyer and not with the outside attorney directly. For many attorneys in large law firms there is

22. Phil E. Gilbert, jr.: 'Joint Responsibility: Corporate Counsel and Retained Counsel', American Bar Association Journal, August 1956, pp. 715-719.

a basic difference between representing a company with a legal staff and representing an individual client. The attorney has a primary responsibility to the company lawyer who is the channel through whom communications with the client on matters of litigation must always be funneled. On the other hand the company lawyer is responsible to see that the attorney representing the company receives all information necessary for this case.

3. Another field where the close cooperation between company lawyer and outside attorney can be advantageous are cases of product liability. Normally claims based on product liability are first reported by the sales department to the legal department. Here the claims are studied and by questioning sales personnel and manufacturing personnel a first opinion is developed as to whether the company is liable for the damages claimed or not. Then, the claim is reported to the insurance company. Often the insurance company readily accepts the assistance and cooperation of the company because only the company has the technical expertise concerning the product involved which is necessary to build up a proper defense. The company lawyer collects all the information required and finally selects − in agreement and after consultation with the insurance company − an experienced outside attorney to represent the company in this case. Thereafter, all information is handed over to the outside attorney and after he has studied the material he is briefed by experts of the company in conferences which are arranged by the company lawyer on the various aspects of the case. It would be very difficult for the outside attorney himself to collect this expertise in the company because he does not know where to dig and whom to contact. Thereafter the law suit takes its time and the company lawyer follows closely the argumentation used by the opponent as well as by the company's attorney te make sure that his statements can be supported by company expertise.

4. Most agencies and branches of government are worlds in themselves. In these organizations one has to deal with a closely knit group of specialists and, therefore, it is advisable to use specialized outside counsel who practises regularly before these agencies and who has made this speciality a full-time job. There are fields in which the specialist who deals with such problems constantly under a variety of situations can develop an expertise that one cannot expect to find in a company legal department unless that type of problem is faced by the legal department regularly. The specialist has the contacts and knows the personnel involved in the agency, as well as the precedence; therefore, he can deal much more effectively with such cases than members of the legal department who do not have this experience. The company lawyer knows the information sources, collects the material and prepares the facts (for instance market shares of products in procedures before antitrust or cartel authorities). He can then present the specialist with information in such a way that the specialist is able to deal with the regulatory agencies of government out of a position of full knowledge and expert evaluation of the facts.

5. Whenever legal work arises in communities far away from company headquarters and the domicile of the company legal department, outside counsel has to be used. The local counsel knows the local personalities in and out of the court room and he is familiar with regional customs and prejudices, he has local contacts and therefore better opportunities than a counsel coming from an out of town company law department. Therefore many companies have built up a net of outside attorneys in locations where from time to time cases come up. In almost every large city there are attorneys with outstanding abilities in certain specific areas of work. It would be unwise not to take advantage of these local attorneys.

6. More and more, company lawyers become involved in international legal work. Large companies expand their activities into other countries either by the establishment of foreign affiliates, the acquisition of existing companies or part of the shares of such companies, or at least by building up an export business. For the company legal department, it is impossible to have detailed and expert knowledge of the laws of all countries where such company activities are commenced. In many countries, also language problems prevent the company lawyer from studying the local legislative system himself. In these cases he acts as a kind of coordinator between the legal system of the home-country and the foreign legal system. He has to make sure that both systems can be harmonized and that the activity of any branch of the company does not result in problems for the remainder of the company. To understand the foreign legal system, the very first step necessary in a new geographical area is to find a local attorney who is experienced in dealing with foreign investments and who speaks a language which the company lawyer commands. In most countries, especially developing countries this will be English. Frequently, this lawyer will advise the newcomer firm not only in legal matters but also other matters.

During the partnership partners meet regularly in the presence of a local attorney to whom both parties have confidence and who can act as adviser to the joint venture as well as to the two parties holding the shares of the joint venture. He can explain to the foreign partner the situation and necessities of the host country. Often he also will represent the foreign partner on the board of directors of the joint venture or its equivalent especially in countries where by law nationals have a certain preference for membership in such institutions. The local manager who often is a foreigner can consult the attorney in all legal, but also local and economic questions.

Summing up it can be stated that the relationship between outside attorneys and companies has been improved and intensified since the advent of the company legal department. His role for the company has become more effective because his colleagues in the legal department are better able to utilize his expertise than management personnel. The combination of outside counsel and company lawyer gives the company the best legal protection and guidance. Jointly, they can make valuable contributions to the work of the company.

E. The Role of the Large American Law Firms

A remarkable phenomenon of legal life in the United States are the large American law firms, which do not have something comparable in Europe (a well known German Rechtsanwalt, Dr. Walter Oppenhof, called Germany in this respect a 'developing country').

The relationship between house-counsel and outside lawyer has been strongly influenced by these large American law firms. They originally were the legal advisers of the large American corporations. Their influence has not suffered from the rise of the company legal departments; maybe it has even grown. When a large Wall Street law firm becomes counsel to a corporation, a senior partner generally will become a member of its board of directors, a junior partner will become its General Counsel and his associates often become members of the legal department: The old team is still working together only the titles have changed.[23] For Europeans it is difficult to imagine the influence and importance of these law firms, because one hardly finds such big law firms outside of the United States. The British Inns of Court in London may rank with Wall Street law firms in tradition and prestige, but these U.S. firms command, in addition, remarkable influence, power and money. This influence extends far beyond the economic life, into politics and government agencies. They affect public policy when it is being shaped by Congress or the regulatory agencies. Their partners move into government positions and return afterwards to their law firms, thus strengthening its influence.[24] It is customary for American companies to work with an outside law firm regularly and one often can find in the annual reports partners of these firms listed as members of the board of directors. If a large corporation turns over an important case to another law firm, it can be sure that the public takes notice of this decision and that speculations as to the reason for this unusual move will rise.[25] Despite the loss of market shares to the competition – the company legal departments and out-of-town firms – the Wall Street firms have grown considerably partly because of new kinds of law which became important for the corporations.[26] Following the expansion of their clients activities into foreign countries, many American law firms opened offices abroad, mostly in London, Paris and Brussels.[27]

If required, these offices put at the disposal of American affiliated companies in Europe the same kind of legal service, which the parent company enjoys with the Wall Street firm. Multinational operations expanded the size of the

23. Paul Hoffman, op. cit., p. 77.
24. Joseph C. Goulden: 'The Superlawyers', New York 1972.
25. Walter Kiechel: 'The Strange Case of Kodak's Lawyers', Fortune May 8, 1978 and 'Growing Up at Kutak Rock & Huie', Fortune October 23, 1978.
26. Peter W. Bernstein: 'The Wall Street Lawyers are thriving on Change', Fortune March 13, 1978.
27. James J. Johnson: 'The Foreign Offices of American Law Firms', Unpublished Paper delivered at the American Branch of the International Law Association, New York April 12, 1978.

law firms and their internal organization became more complex. It is obvious that the employment of 200 and more lawyers in some of the largest firms created management problems which apparently have been solved.[28] It cannot be denied that the law firms serve their clients and help them defend themselves against courts, laws and administrative agencies which, particularly in the last quarter-century, expanded their regulatory activities into formerly unknown dimensions. Lawyers became indispensable and this irritates layman.[29] The famous line from Shakespeare's Henry VI, Second Part, IV., 2: 'The first thing we do, let's kill all the lawyers', is quoted again, but it certainly will not hurt the business of the Wall Street law firms, which have become an indispensable part of the American company law praxis. Because of their experience and expertise, they are the counterparts of the company legal departments.

F. Lawyers as Members of Board of Directors

As mentioned before in the United States members of large law firms serve often on board of directors of companies which their law firms have as client. One of the most interesting surveys and studies about attorneys who serve as outside legal counsel and director of corporations has been published by the Law Journal Press in the publication 'Outside Counsel − Inside Director' (The Directory of Lawyers on the Boards of American Industry, 1976, revised edition, Law Journal Press 1977). The information covers more than 1100 law firms and approximately 1800 corporations. The authors found that apparently some of the big law firms discourage their partners from serving on boards of corporations, because of recent court decisions which expand the potential liability of outside corporate directors. But also in Europe lawyers are frequently members of supervisory boards (Aufsichtsräte) and similar institutions. In the Federal Republic of Germany the various codetermination acts and the increase in size of supervisory boards has brought many Rechtsanwälte into the position of alternate member of the board. This is not limited to practising lawyers but also members of the bar who are in permanent employment have been appointed to such positions. The duties and responsibilities of the members of board of directors or supervisory boards are regulated under local laws but certain factors which apply specifically to lawyers acting as directors require study and if possible uniform rules of the legal profession. Therefore, the International Bar Association has studied the problems facing lawyers in various countries when serving as directors of companies and the Counsel of the International Bar Association authorized on April 22, 1978 'A Practical Guide to the Conduct of Lawyer Directors'.[30] The guide covers

28. Daniel J. Cantor: 'Law Firms are Getting Bigger . . . and More Complex', American Bar Association Journal February 1978, pp. 215-219.
29. 'Those Lawyers', Time April 10, 1978, pp. 50-55.
30. International Bar Journal, May 1978, pp. 33-40.

primarily the position of practising lawyers who serve as non-executive directors on the boards of companies. It touches less directly the position of lawyers in those countries where they are allowed, without losing their professional qualifications, to be salaried employees and who become directors, executive or not, of companies in the group which employs them. If they become members of board of directors or supervisory boards outside the group which employs them the same principles apply as those for practising lawyers. Conflicts are not so likely in countries where the two-tier board structure is used (Germany and the Netherlands are the best known examples). The conflict situation for the lawyer-director between his duties as director and his duties as lawyer is reduced. Nevertheless, such conflict situation can arise, if a lawyer having a seat in a supervisory board or a board of directors is at the same time the legal adviser of the company. The guide states that the two-tier structure (where available) makes it easier for a lawyer who is offered a seat on a supervisory board.

Similar principles apply according to art. 17 of the guide to a salaried lawyer on the staff of a company:

'Inside-Counsel

> Similar principles apply to a salaried lawyer on the staff of a company. He should carefully weigh the advantages and disadvantages of becoming a director of the company itself or of its subsidiaries while at the same time acting as legal adviser. This position may well be more difficult than that of an independent lawyer-director. As a lawyer himself the inside-counsel will wish so far as possible to protect his professional independence and integrity. He may, however, when there is divergence of view on matters where he is seeking to preserve that integrity, be faced with the stern reality of the fact that he is in salaried employment on which his livelihood and family depend; in such case there may be overwhelming pressure on him to retreat from independent stand-point which the outside lawyer is always free to adopt. The latter may stand to lose a client, the former his job.'

These words show very briefly the problems for company lawyers who serve on boards within their group of companies. Especially if they are appointed to the boards of subsidiaries in foreign countries it will always be a problem how far they get involved in the business affairs of these affiliates. Sometimes a certain number of members is required under local law and it is, therefore, an obvious solution to appoint among others the chief legal adviser of the parent company as a member of the board of the affiliated company. Since his business responsibility can only be very limited the flow of information sometimes also will be very limited. He has to make the decision for himself whether he accepts a nomination of this kind or prefers to maintain his professional independence with the authorities of the host country of the affiliated company. Especially in cases where the affiliated company knowingly or unknowingly has committed a violation of regulations and rules existing in the host country. Therefore, the company lawyer who is appointed to a board within his group of companies should insist on full information also in business matters concerning this affiliated company so that he can be sure that his professional integrity is not teinted by events beyond his control which happen in the affiliated company. If such events happen he serves the parent company better by not being on a board.

IV. The Situation of Company Lawyers in Various Countries

In most European countries the regulations for the admission of jurists to the Bar prohibit the admission of jurists in permanent employment. The underlying principle is that an attorney at law should be independent in order to be able to represent his clients. This is not the place to discuss this principle but besides in the United States of America only in the United Kingdom and the Federal Republic of Germany jurists permanently employed by an enterprise can be admitted to the Bar.

This situation has deprived company lawyers in the other countries of the membership in a professional organization. It is, therefore, not surprising that in most of these countries company jurists have established associations to represent their interests and to further contacts among themselves. I shall try hereinafter to list some specifics existing in the various countries:

A. Australia

In Australia company legal departments are growing in size and in number. The typical company having its own legal department is the affiliated company of a foreign based multinational company. Here the influence of the foreign parent company which is used to have its own legal department becomes obvious. But also large Australian companies are having more and more their own legal department which sometimes can be as strong as any which we know in Europe or the United States of America. Especially strong are legal departments in the oil and mining industries, where not only the acquisition and sale of land and property is important but also environmental problems and governmental negotiations can be very time-consuming. Therefore, in this industry more lawyers are employed than in other industries. It is estimated that there are approximately 200 company legal departments existing in Australia with a total number of up to 1000 lawyers in permanent employ. The number of legal departments and company lawyers is fast growing, partly because government overregulates industry.

B. Austria

In Austria it is not possible to be a member of the Bar and to be permanently employed by a company. Therefore, company jurists are part of the hierarchical system of their company. It is surprising that in Austria no special 'legal' titles are used but instead management titles are used. Within the company the person in charge of the legal department carries the title 'Leiter der Rechtsabteilung'. Within the hierarchical structure of the company heads of legal departments are 'Prokurist' of their company. But there are also cases where the head of the legal department is a member of the management board of the company. Legal departments report in almost all cases directly to the head of the company, i.e. 'Vorstand' or 'Geschäftsführer'. The size of the legal departments differs, but normally they do not have more than 5 jurists.

C. Belgium

1. For the preparation of a seminar organized by the University of Liège in 1967 on the subject 'Juriste d'Entreprise' a questionnaire has been sent to 47 large Belgian enterprises which have a legal department. In these 47 companies 720 'Docteur en Droit' were employed, but apparently only 124 of them did purely legal work. The other jurists worked in other departments of the company especially financial departments or in administrative departments.[1] Even in companies where jurists were employed in legal work, the institutionalization of company legal departments had not always taken place at the time the questions were answered. The jurist often was attached to some other department even though he was dealing primarily with legal problems especially in smaller companies. The evaluation of questionnaires sent out by the Commission Droit et Vie des Affaires in 1965 showed that in responding 80 companies 11 jurists were in charge or supervising organizations which included the legal department, 15 were in charge of legal departments employing more than 1 jurist, 7 were members of a legal department with more than 1 jurist and 13 mentioned as their sole occupation to direct a legal department, 23 did legal work besides other matters and 11 did not work in legal matters.[2] The responses received do not reflect the importance of legal departments in Belgium. One third of the industrial enterprises questioned having more than 1000 employees do not have a separate legal department. Their legal matters are handled by a jurist who has also other responsibilities. Legal departments in larger Belgian companies are not as far developed as in other industrialized countries. Out of 80 enterprises involved in the study 15 had jurists before 1945 but only after 1955 the larger number of these companies has established legal departments.

1. Maurice-André Flamme, 'Le Role et les Fonctions du Juriste d'Entreprise', Le Jurist d'Entreprise, p. 28.
2. 'La Fonction du Juriste d'Entreprise en Belgique', Le Juriste d'Entreprise, p. 54.

2. The title most often used for the legal department is 'Service Juridique' or 'Département Juridique'. The jurist in charge of the legal department has the title 'Chef' or 'Directeur du Service Juridique'. Members are called 'Attaché au Service Juridique' or 'Conseil Juridique'.

The jurist in charge of the legal department in most companies reports directly to the 'Président Directeur Général' or the 'Administrateur Délégué'. (Both positions are the equivalent of the American 'Chief Executive Officer'). In some companies he reports to the 'Administrative Directeur' but in those cases he is not working full-time for legal matters but has other tasks.

3. Belgian company jurists cannot be admitted to the Bar because article 437, 4° du Code Judicière − Tome III 'On Members of the Bar' states that jurists who are in a paid public or private employment cannot be admitted to the Bar except if their independence as attorney or their ethical situation as attorney is not endangered. This legislation wants to ensure the independence of the attorneys at law. In a 'Résolution relative à l'exercise par les stagières de certaines activités professionelles extérieures au barreau' which was published on January 25, 1977, a slight modification of this attitude can be noted. Referring to articles 435 and 456 of the Code Judicière this resolution states that it is difficult for a great number of attorneys in training to find places where they can be trained. In view of this situation the principles of the Bar can authorize a jurist in training to exercise an activity outside of the Bar for training reasons or to have a supplemental income, if this activity does not endanger the independence of the attorney or the dignity of the Bar. This activity can also be a remunerated public or private employment. It may not extend for more than one year. The person in training continues to belong to his profession, i.e. attorney-at-law and his additional employment must permit him to exercise his functions as member of the Bar.

This order of the Conseil de l'Ordre du Barreau de Bruxelles has found in Belgian industry some attention. The Employers' Federation of Belgium commented on it[3] and remembers that the attorney-at-law thus employed in an enterprise is not permitted to represent his own company before the courts. The federation finds this move encouraging because it offers to the young jurists the opportunity to become familiar with the economic and social mecanisms in an enterprise.

4. In 1968 Belgian company lawyers founded 'L'Association Belge des Juristes d'Entreprise − 'Belgische Vereniging van Bedrijfsjuristen'. The foundation of this organization was formalized on September 8, 1970, and its statutes were published in 'Moniteur Belge' on December 17, 1970.[4] Object of the organization is to organize company jurists to advise and work out opinions on interesting legal or business matters, to further the post-

3. Bulletin No. 21, Sept. 1, 1977 − p. 2609/10.
4. No. 7270.

graduate education of its members especially by centralized documentation, publications, exchange of experiences, seminars etc. Its members have to obey the professional code of ethics. Contacts with Belgian and foreign professional organizations is one of the purposes and it wants in general to develop the situation and position of the company lawyer and to define his position in relation to the other branches of the legal profession, in business and social life. The organization does not want to act as a 'trade union' of the company lawyers.

Article 5 states as condition for membership that members can be 'Docteur en Droit' or 'Licencié en Droit' or public notaries who have practised law at least five years, who exercise legal functions in an enterprise and who are recognized by the association as having the quality of company lawyer.

The association has some three hundred members who represent more than 80 of the largest Belgian companies and organizations. It organizes conferences which find wide attention. These conferences deal with various legal problems which are of importance for companies or their legal departments. A number of publications have resulted from the activity of the association, some of these were published in connection with the University of Liège. In relatively short time, the association has become an important part of the legal profession in Belgium.

D. Federal Republic of Germany

1. Exact figures concerning the number of jurists in permanent employment for companies or business or trade organizations do not exist. Estimates concerning the number of jurists in industry were about 3,000 (3,2% of the total legal personnel) in 1970. In a not specified position of 'other employment' an additional 6,600 (7,1%) were mentioned. The number of attorneys-at-law was 41,000 (43,8%) and it can be assumed that also in this figure a considerable number of persons in permanent employment is included.[5] In a reply given to the Deutsche Bundestag on June 6, 1977, the Federal Minister of Justice could not state exactly how many jurists are employed by business or other associations.[6] The magazin 'Capital' estimates that 10,000 jurists are employed in German industry, commerce and associations (10/78, page 325). This lack of exact figures can be explained by the fact that most company lawyers in the Federal Republic of Germany are members of the bar (Rechtsanwälte) and therefore included in the figures for Rechtsanwälte. There are

5. Unpublished report of Dr. Hans Dichgans, dated September 4, 1975 concerning the education of Wirtschafsjuristen (jurists in business). These figures are based on information given by the German Ministry of Education and Science.
6. Deutscher Bundestag, Drucksache 8/550. Wolfgang Fröhlich mentioned in 1968 a number of 12000 and more jurists employed in industry and trade of which between 5000 and 6000 were Rechtsanwälte (Le Statut du Juriste d'Entreprise en République Fédérale d'Allemagne, Le Juriste d'Entreprise, pp. 91-101).

estimates that up to one third of all German Rechtsanwälte are in permanent employment either with a company or a business organization. Alle large and many smaller companies have their own legal departments. A considerable number of jurists is furthermore working in patent and trade mark departments, tax departments and personnel departments of companies.

Ruschemeyer estimates in his comparative study of the legal profession in Germany and in the United States that the proportion of lawyers among business executives is about 6% in the United States and 6 to 8% in Germany. The proportion increases considerably when executives of the largest firms only are considered. In this case 15% of American business leaders in this category and 21% of their German counterparts were lawyers.[7] A very strong position have lawyers in business associations. Many employed Rechtsanwälte are on the staff of German business associations and the legal departments of the various great associations cooperate closely with house counsel of affiliated firms.

2. Legal departments are called 'Rechtsabteilung', 'Ressort Recht' or some similar denomination which is in connection with the word law. The jurist in charge of the legal department in many companies has the title 'Chefjustitiar', 'Chefsyndikus' or 'Leiter der Rechtsabteilung'.

The lawyer in charge of the legal department is frequently, especially in large companies a member of the management board (Vorstand or Geschäftsführung). If that is not the case, he reports directly to the President of the company (Vorsitzender des Vorstandes) and has as rank often the title 'Generalbevollmächtigter'. This incidates that he is immediately below the Board of Management.[8]

3. Under German legislation a jurist in permanent employment can be admitted to the bar if the employment does not impair his independence as Rechtsanwalt. This principle of 'Freiheit der Advokatur' (Freedom of advocacy) is the underlying principle of the profession in Germany and it is based on ideas of the French revolution. The Rechtsanwalt is an 'independent organ of the administration of justice' (unabhängiges Organ der Rechtspflege, § 1b Bundesrechtsanwaltsordnung). He has to advise and represent his clients independently (§ 3 Abs. 1 BRAO).

One guiding principle of German legal ethics is that the role of the Rechtsanwalt must be one's primary occupation and cannot be taken on as a sideline. Any occupation that interferes with the independence of the Bar is considered incompatible. House counsel can be admitted to the Bar only if the character of his position guarantees the required independence. Also the house counsel who has been admitted to the Bar has duties to his profession. Four basic obligations of the Rechtsanwalt, whether he is in permanent employment or not, exist: to be loyal to the law and the administration of justice, to be loyal

7. Rueschemeyer, op. cit., p. 78.
8. Hans Dichgans, op. cit., p. 5.

to his client, to be loyal to his colleagues and their professional community, and to maintain his independent freedom of judgment and decision.

Between the end of the First World War and 1930 more and more companies established their own legal departments which were directed mostly by former outside counsel. Therefore the German Bar discussed whether a Rechtsanwalt can be in permanent employment. This question was answered in the affirmative by the special courts supervising the ethical conduct of Rechtsanwälte.

The Bundesrechtsanwaltsordnung dated August 1, 1959 states in § 46 that a Rechtsanwalt cannot represent his employer before courts or arbitration courts in his capacity as Rechtsanwalt. With this limitation the institution of the employed Rechtsanwalt (Syndikusanwalt) has been acknowledged.[9] In Continental Europe German company lawyers are the only ones who can be as Rechtsanwälte part of the advocacy.

4. In 1978 the Deutsche Anwaltsverein (the organization of the German Rechtsanwälte) invited company lawyers who are Rechtsanwalt to form their own organization. This took place in the form of the 'Arbeitsgemeinschaft der Syndikusanwälte im Deutschen Anwaltsverein'. The organization has the purpose to further the interests of Rechtsanwälte in permanent employment and to promote the study of fields of law which are of special interest for company lawyers. The Arbeitsgemeinschaft has at the time at which this article is written approximately 200 members.

E. France

1. The position of French company lawyers is not very strong. Only few enterprises have conseillers juridiques as members of their top management and decisions very seldom are seriously studied under legal aspects. The service juridique of French companies primarily defends lawsuits. Preventive law is only seldom entrusted to the company legal department. The reason for this development can be traditional because in a period of liberalism the law had not penetrated as strongly as today the business of companies.[10] There exist no estimates of the numbers of jurists employed by French companies.

2. The titles most often used are 'service juridique', 'service légal', 'service contentieux' etc. [11]

9. Fritz Börtzler, 'Der Syndikusanwalt', Ehrengabe für Bruno Heusinger, München 1968, pp. 119-140.
10. M. Demay and M. Rivero, 'L'Entreprise et le Juriste', Patronat Français No. 276, August-September 1967, pp. 6-11.
11. 'Le Statut du Juriste d'Entreprise en France', par la Délégation Française, Le Juriste d'Entreprise, pp. 135-144.

3. Until recently company lawyers could not be members of the French Bar. Until December 31, 1971 they were even 'ignored' by the law.[12] The new legislation is very important for French company lawyers because in the discussions before and the deliberations of the law at one time it was proposed to prohibit enterprises to employ jurists for certain types of legal work. The new law for the first time recognizes the existence of the company lawyers. The text of the law does not mention the company lawyer but in a circulaire of October 16, 1972 concerning the conseiller juridique certain equivalent working times for gaining practical experiences are listed, which are required to become a conseiller juridique. In these examples also the work in a service juridique of a company is expressly listed.[13] The second step is a new décret no 78/1081 of November 13, 1978 on the legal profession. In part 44-1 juristes d'entreprise are especially mentioned because it is stated that former company lawyers who have at least 8 years of practical experience can be admitted to the Bar without additional formal education. Company lawyers in the meaning of this clause are those jurists who work exclusively in company legal departments or tax departments of enterprises which employ at least three jurists.

4. In 1969 'L'Association Française des Juristes d'Entreprises' was founded in Paris. The foundation was an act of defence because a number of outside counsels at that time had voiced the idea that legal problems of companies should be dealt with exclusively by advocats. Therefore, the foundation of the French Company Lawyer Association can be seen as a way to unite French company lawyers and to give them more strength in presenting their opinion to the public. The association has very successfully worked in educating its members in certain fields of economic law. It has assisted in the creation of special courses in three French legal faculties, namely in Aix-en-Provence, Montpellier and Rennes where special diplomas as juristes d'entreprises can be obtained. Together with universities a number of symposia has been organized. The association has now approximately 300 members.

F. Italy

1. Italian estimates speak of approximately 250 company lawyers employed in industry (without banks and insurance companies) who do legal work only. Definite figures are not available, though. Some Italian sources relate the number of company lawyers employed in the law department of an enterprise to the turnover of the company. The Italian Company Lawyers' Association developed statistics according to which with a turnover of Lira 9000 Billion

12. Xavier de Mello, 'L'Association Française des Juristes d'Entreprise et le Juriste d'Entreprise', Conférence prononcée à Milan le 15 Octobre 1977, mimeographed.
13. 'Professions Judiciaires et Juridiques', Journal Officiel de la République Française, 1974, p. 270.

ENI employs 80 lawyers. Olivetti with a turnover between Lira 1000 Billions and 2000 Billions has 10 lawyers in the company's legal department. Especially large are the legal departments of subsidiaries of American companies operating in Italy. The legal department reports normally directly to the President of the company.

The title used for the head of the legal department is 'responsabile affari legali' or 'direttore servici legali'. Company lawyers have in many companies the formal position of 'segretario del consiglio dei amministrazione'.

Until recently the company lawyer was only dealing with outstanding debts and tax problems. He was not the legal adviser whom we know from other countries. All cases of some importance and contracts were handled by outside lawyers. The company lawyer was a kind of controller for legal matters, i.e. he merely controlled whether decisions made in the enterprise were not in conflict with legal regulations. This situation is rapidly changing. Company lawyers now are entrusted with more and more responsibility and preventive law is being practised by the legal departments, especially in large Italian companies. Strongly involved are company legal departments in matters of labour law, a result of the Italian labour law system which is splitted in many regulations. Also the difficulties in dealing with Italian trade unions have influenced this development. In general it can be stated that Italian legal departments are gaining importance and that their work load is increasing steadily because of the volume of legislation and the severe criminal responsibilities of management under Italian law.

2. The profession of attorney-at-law is regulated in Italy by law no. 36 of January 22, 1934. Under this law it is not possible for jurists in permanent employment to be inscribed in the 'Albo deggli avvocati'. Excepted from this restriction are lawyers working in law departments of public institutions or organizations. The best known exception is probably Internazionale Hydrocarburi (ENI), where company lawyers in permanent employment are permitted to be avvocati and to represent this institution before the courts.[14]

3. In June 1976 the 'Assoziazione Italiana Giuristi d'Impresa (AIGI)' was founded in Milano as organization of Italian company lawyers. The statute of AIGI defines in art. 1 the activity of the Giurista d'Impresa as recognition and solving of legal problems of the company and advising and assisting in the decision-making process in the company. Objective of the association is according to art. 3 the information and assistance of its members by exchange of experiences and the organization of congresses, conventions to facilitate such exchange of experiences. The AIGI has at present approximately 80 members who are of the opinion that it is most important for them to exchange freely ideas with colleagues who also work in industry and that it is necessary

14. 'La Fonction du Juriste d'Entreprise en Italie', par le Groupe de Travail Italien, Le Juriste d'Entreprise, pp. 145-149.

to communicate with each other especially concerning legal problems which are typical for industrial companies. They are convinced that in the legal departments of Italian companies there are specialists for fields which can be found very seldom outside of large companies.

The association maintains contacts with Italian and foreign professional organizations especially with those existing within the Common Market. Members of the association can be all persons with an examination in law and who are in permanent employment as company lawyer in Italian companies. One condition is that the member is more than 5 years working as a company lawyer. So-called 'aderenti' members can be those with less than 5 years professional experience. One of the reasons for the strong interest to exchange professional experiences between the members is the 'chaotic' Italian legislation which according to the members makes it difficult to judge correctly the cases.[15]

G. Luxemburg

1. Only very few large companies in Luxemburg have their own 'service juridique'. These legal departments occupy themselves with all legal problems of the company. The titles used are 'Directeur du Contentieux', 'Conseillé', 'Chef de Service', 'Attaché'. Companies also employ Docteurs en Droit who work not only in legal matters but also in administrative and commercial matters. Then hierarchical titles used are 'Sécretaire Général', 'Chef de Service', 'Fondé de Pouvoir'.

2. The legal profession is regulated in Luxemburg by a decret of 1801. This statute of the profession of avocat states in art. 18 that the profession is incompatible with permanent employment. Therefore company lawyers cannot be inscribed into the 'tableau des avocats' of the 'Conseil de l'ordre des avocats'. Professional organizations of company lawyers do not exist in Luxemburg.[16]

H. The Netherlands

1. Company lawyers are employed by the large international companies in Holland since more than 50 years. Therefore, this part of the legal profession has organized itself more firmly than in most other European countries. The large international companies (i.e. Unilever, Philips, etc.) have contributed considerably to the development of this part of the Dutch legal profession. Company lawyers in Holland are only those jurists who do legal work full time

15. Fabio Galli, 'In ditta è la legge il mio mestiere', Espansione No. 94, November 1977.
16. 'La Fonction du Juriste d'Entreprise au Grand-Duché de Luxembourg', par la Délégation Luxembourgeoise, Le Juriste d'Entreprise, pp. 151-155.

in a company legal department.[17] The Dutch term used is 'Bedrijfsjurist' or 'Juridisch Adviseur'. The head of the legal department is called 'Hoofd afd. juridische Zaken' or 'Hoofd juridische Afdeling'. Though the head of the law department is not an officer of the company himself, he reports either directly to the president or to the board of the company.

In Holland company lawyers cannot be admitted to the Bar. Therefore they cannot represent their company before law courts. This had resulted in a close cooperation between company lawyers and free practising lawyers.

2. In Sepember 1975 the Dutch organization of company lawyers to which I shall refer later on published an enquete conducted by Mr. J. van den Berg on the situation of the company lawyer in Dutch companies.[18] In this enquete 216 companies participated and 84 companies replied to a questionnaire which the organization had worked out. Two thirds of the participating companies belong to the large Dutch companies, 63% had 2000 employees or more. The evaluation of this enquete defines company lawyer as a 'jurist who does primarily legal work in a company'. A different position has a jurist in the company, i.e. a jurist who is also permanently employed by a company but who does not primarily legal work.[19] It is interesting that of the companies with less than 2000 employees, 46,5% had a legal department and of the companies with more than 2000 employees even 94,3% had an own legal department. This shows the longstanding history and importance of legal departments in Holland. The legal departments have between 1 and 55 employees. 17% of the departments existed already before 1945. Another 17% were established between 1945 and 1959. In 90% of all cases the head of the legal department reported directly to the top management of the company.

Interesting is also the break-down by percentages of the fields of law dealt with in the company legal departments of the companies which answered the questionnaire. This break-down shows that for instance company law is dealt with by more than 77% of the legal departments without any help either from outside or inside the company. On the other hand consumer law was dealt with by only 4,3% of the legal departments questioned. In 95% of the companies this matter was not coming up. Definitely this would have changed if the enquete was done again today. The largest percentage of work given outside of the company was industrial property, which 44% handled solely in the legal department, 30% in connection with other departments of the company and 10% completely outside of the company.

3. Also in the Netherlands no definite figures are available concerning the number of jurists working in industry. An enquete held in 1972 estimated that

17. Wolf, Drion, Jitta, Koomans & Rogmans, 'La Fonction et la Position du Juriste d'Entreprise Néerlandais', Le Juriste d'Entreprise, pp. 157-172.
18. J.W.M. van den Berg, 'De Bedrijfsjurist', September 1975, mimeographed.
19. Op. cit., p. 11.

4200 jurists were employed in industry out of a total of 12500 jurists in Holland. But only part of these jurists works in company legal departments. This estimate comes also to the conclusion that 830 company lawyers are working as what is called 'generalists' and 460 as company lawyers specialized in legal departments. This would result in a total of 1290 lawyers in Dutch legal departments, a considerable number in relation to the size of the country.

This enquete is very important because it is until now probably the most thoroughly conducted sociological research concerning position and number of company lawyers.

4. The organization which conducted this investigation is 'Het Nederlands Genootschap van Bedrijfsjuristen' (N.G.B.). This organization was founded already in 1930 and therefore, is the oldest specialized organization of company lawyers in the world. The association was founded on October 10, 1930 under the name 'Studiegezelschap van Juristen, Werkzaam bij Handel en Industrie'. In 1938 the organization had 50 members. The association has at present approximately 210 members.

The statute of the association states in Art. 2 that the purpose is to further the legal sciences and law practice in connection with commercial life. This object is reached among other things by general assemblies of the members, conduct of studies and advice. Art. 5 requires that ordinary members have the legal education of a Meester in de Rechten by passing the doctor examination at a Dutch university. They must be employed in a legal personality in the Netherlands which is active in private business. His major working time must be devoted to the activity as company lawyer and he must have this position for a certain period of time, which normally should not be less than two years. The importance of the organization is not only documented by the above mentioned sociological report on the situation of company lawyers in Holland but also by the fact that since 1946 more than 150 seminars have been held by the organization. All these seminars have dealt with legal subjects which are of importance for company lawyers.[20]

I. Sweden

1. According to recent estimates there are about 300 company lawyers in Sweden. The company lawyer has a long standing history because already at the end of the last century there were company legal departments existing, but only after the Second World War the number increased considerably.[21]

2. The heads of company legal departments in Sweden have often the title

20. Ter Kennismaking, N.G.B. 1972, pp. 9-12.
21. B. Akeson, 'Considérations sur le Statut et le Role du Juriste d'Entreprise en Suède', Le Juriste d'Entreprise, pp. 173-182.

'Ombudsman', but today also frequently 'Chefs-Jurist'. Members of company legal departments are called often 'Bolags-Jurist'.

3. Company lawyers cannot be members of the Bar, but on the other hand Swedish lawyers are not the only ones, who can appear before the court, but every person who has had a legal training is authorized to plead before the court. The title 'Advokat' is reserved to members of the Sveriges Advokatsamfund. The Swedish company lawyer therefore is not compelled to turn over a matter to an advokat if litigation must be expected.

4. In 1954 the Swedish Association of Company Lawyers ('Bolagsjuristernasförening') was founded. Its most important object is to constitute a forum for company lawyers where they can exchange experiences. The association has contributed positively to the solidarity of the company lawyers in Sweden.[22] The membership is at present 250.
In addition there exists a section in Jurist- och Samhällsvetareförbundet (JUS) which is part of the Swedish Confederation of Professional Association. This organization takes care of the professional problems of company lawyers as there are salary problems and other economic questions, etc.

J. United Kingdom

1. The number of barristers and solicitors in permanent employ in the legal department of private corporations has increased considerably. In 1961 it was estimated that between 350 and 400 lawyers were employed by private corporations in legal departments.[23] In 1967 no trade union had a legal staff or even a salaried lawyer employed as such.[24] In 1978, 650 barristers belonged to the Bar Association for Commerce, Finance and Industry, which represents the interests of the employed barristers. Solicitors in business are about 2500.[25]

2. Considering company lawyers in England one must first of all keep in mind that the legal profession in England is divided into the two branches, barrister and solicitor. These two branches have independent histories, reaching back probably to the 13th century. By definition a barrister is the advocate or trial lawyer, who's primary function is the presentation of cases in court and the solicitor is the person who deals with the paperwork, the preparation of litigation and who handles all non-litigious legal matters. He is in direct touch with the client.[26] A solicitor acting as a company lawyer is regarded as being

22. Op. cit., p. 174.
23. D. Rowe, 'The Lawyer in Industry', Times Review of Industry, June 1961.
24. Quintin Johnstone and Dan Hopson, Jr., op. cit. p. 377.
25. Neil Crichton-Miller, 'Lawyers in Business', Sunday Telegraph, April 30, 1978.
26. Clifford W.R. Edwards, 'Industry's Use of the Lawyer in England', The Business Lawyer, November 1960, pp. 124-133.

in practice and he has, of course, to obey the rules set out by the Law Society, but he is in precisely the same position as he would be as if he were in practice. This has considerable importance concerning the position of company lawyers in English companies. It results in a tendency to organize the legal department on a solicitor/client basis and the activities of the department normally comprise all the functions of a solicitor's office. This includes instruction of counsel (barrister) if necessary. Company lawyers in England have a tendency to make sure that their position both relative to the client and professionally corresponds as closely as possible with that of the lawyer in private practice. Therefore, a clear differentiation exists between legal advice and management decisions. Maintaining the professional position and responsibility has important practical consequences because in a decision of 1974 the House of Lords recognized that the legal professional privilege could in certain circumstances attach to communications between an organization and its internal legal advisers.[27]

Many legal departments are staffed by barristers and solicitors working together as colleagues.[28] But the barrister is in a more difficult position than the solicitor who is considered as being in practice. Barristers in permanent employ may not instruct practising barristers without the intervention of a solicitor. They may not act for their employers in certain matters. They may not act as an advocate in court and furthermore they may not use in correspondence or other documents the title 'Barrister-at-Law'.[29]

3. According to the division of the legal profession also for English company lawyers there exist two organizations. The organization of solicitors in England is The Law Society. It has a 'Commerce and Industry Group', members of which are the members of the Law Society who are employed in commerce and industry. This group has at present approximately 1150 members. There are, of course, also solicitors working in commerce and industry who are not members of the group. The parallel organization for barristers working in commerce and industry is the 'Bar Association for Commerce, Finance and Industry'. It has about 500 members. Both organizations cooperate very closely and exercise a strong influence within their respective professional groups.

27. Brion J. Youngman, 'Organization and Work of the Legal Department of the National Coal Board in England', International Bar Association Sydney Conference, September 1978, mimeographed.
28. D.G. Fletcher Rogers, 'The Company Lawyer-Etiquette and Ethics', Le Juriste d'Entreprise, pp. 431-438.
29. Brian Russel, 'A Survey of the Function and Position of Company Lawyers in England and Wales', Le Juriste d'Entreprise, pp. 103-112 and M.H. Gow, 'The Ethics of the Company Lawyer', Le Juriste d'Entreprise, pp. 439-445.

K. United States of America

1. I can deal rather briefly with the position of company lawyers in the United States because the literature on this subject has been the basis for most of the explanations given in this paper. The number of company lawyers has increased rapidly during the last 20 years. In 1949 out of 5428 attorneys employed by 2048 private organizations 1996 were employed by a total of 231 industrial corporations having law departments consisting of three or more attorneys. In addition insurance companies employed 895 attorneys and banks 547.[30] In the 1961 Martindale-Hubbell census the number of attorneys serving private industry as full-time counsel was reported as approximately 22500, an increase of 3600 over the past three years.[31] 1963, 26500 lawyers were employed by private industry and this was approximately 11% of all the judges and lawyers in the US.[32]
At present estimates of lawyers employed by company law departments in the US run as high as 40000 lawyers. In Canada the number is relatively small in comparison namely little more than 2000 company lawyers in permanent employment by private industry.

2. The company lawyer's profession in the US has brought about a unique position: the American General Counsel. He is more than the head of the law department but he occupies a position of unusual trust and leadership in most American companies. 'Most General Counsel are concerned as much with political forces outside his company as he is with the economic formation of policy within'.[33] Most of the General Counsel have the status of officer of the company, practically all report directly to the President or Chairman of the Board of their respective companies. A questionnaire quoted by Murphy defines the function of the General Counsel as follows: 'Participation in the top executive and management team of the company with special emphasis on legal matters as they affect corporate policy, direction and planning'.[34] This statement describes very well the unique position which is almost unknown in European companies.

3. In view of the large number and extremely favourable position of company lawyers it is not surprising that strong organizations of company lawyers exist in the US. These organizations further the contact between their members and they have as objective among other things the continuing training of company lawyers in fields of law which are of special importance for the corporations.

30. Charles S. Maddock, op. cit., p. 119.
31. Robert V. Wills, 'A Prenuptial Primer', The Practical Lawyer, March 1962, pp. 49-62.
32. William S. Cummins, 'Status of Corporate Counsel Today', The Business Lawyer, July 1966, pp. 1082-1084.
33. Robert W. Murphy, 'The Profile of a General Counsel, his Position and Function in an American Corporation', Le Juriste d'Entreprise, pp. 117-133.
34. Robert W. Murphy, op. cit., p. 128.

a. The most prestigeous organization is 'The Association of General Counsel'. It was established in 1951 and its objects are to promote high standards of legal service to industrial corporations and to facilitate and promote the study of legal problems of general interest to industrial corporations. Active membership is limited to 75 lawyers who are employed on full-time basis as heads of legal departments of industrial corporations. An Executive Committee decides by majority vote on applications for membership which have to be supported by two active members of the association. The standing of this association is extremely high and the impact of its opinion on legislative projects considerable.

b. Within the American Bar Association's Corporation, Banking and Business Law Section, a Committee on Corporate Law Department exists. The committee meets regularly and discusses problems related to company lawyers and their work. It publishes a 'News for Corporate Counsel' and maintains close relations and contact with law schools.[35] Its most important activity is probably the Annual Corporate Counsel Institute, which is held jointly by Northwestern University School of Law, the Committee on Corporate Law Departments and various State Bar Associations which have also Committees on Corporate Law Departments. This Corporate Counsel Institute is held annually to provide corporate counsel with a broad and expert analysis of current legal problems. Approximately 600 to 650 lawyers from practically all states of the USA and Canada attend the Institute. Other Institutes for corporate counsel are held in New York City regularly.

Another important institution for the continuing education of the legal profession and especially company lawyers is The Southwestern Legal Foundation, International Centre for Advanced Continuing Education, on the Campus of the University of Texas at Dallas. The Foundation was established in 1947 and holds annually numerous seminars on legal subjects. The continuing education of lawyers and company lawyers plays in the US a considerable role and assists in maintaining a high standard of knowledge in specialized fields of law.

L. International Bar Association

The International Bar Association was founded in 1947. Its stated purposes are to establish and maintain permanent relations and exchanges between bar associations throughout the world and their members and to discuss problems of professional organization and status. The IBA has consultative status with the United Nations and the Council of Europe. In 1970 it established a Section on Business Law and in 1974 a Section on General Practice was established at the Vancouver Conference. This section deals primarily with matters

35. Arthur C. O'Meara, 'Committee on Corporate Law Departments, Midyear Report for 1964-1965', The Business Lawyer, April 1965, pp. 802-806.

relating to the general practice of law throughout the world. Both sections have a number of committees. Committee no. 11 (Committee on Corporate Law Departments) of the Section on General Practice was founded in Vancouver 1974.

The Committee on Corporate Law Departments improves the conditions of work and the efficiency of lawyers employed within the legal departments of commercial enterprises, the standing of such lawyers within the hierarchy of the enterprises, including their remunerations. It also studies the conditions of work of such lawyers and their professional liability.

Members of the Committee are approximately 70 company lawyers from companies all over the world.

The Committee has held its first working session at the IBA Conference in Stockholm 1976 and its second working session at the IBA Conference in Sydney 1978. At both working sessions, problems of organization of company legal departments, the role and position of the company lawyer and other questions were discussed on the basis of papers presented by its members.

M. The Company Lawyer in the European Economic Community

The progress of the Common Market, the strengthening of the position and of the activity of the European Commission has had also considerable impact on the activity of company legal departments within the Common Market. New fields of law have been created and play a very important role in the work of company lawyers inside and outside of the memberstates of the Community. The strong influence of these activities resulted among other things in the establishment of the 'Commission Consultative des Barreaux de la Communauté Européenne'. Since 1960 this commission represents the lawyers of the memberstates in contacts with the European Commission and the European Court of Justice.[36]

The European Commission became active regarding the activities of a lawyer from another memberstate rendering services in a state where he is not admitted to the Bar after the European Court of Justice decided in the case Reyners v. Belgium on June 21, 1974 that the Treaty of Rome forbids a host memberstate to discriminate on grounds of nationality in regulating activities of a lawyer from another memberstate.[37] The question to which extent professionals of a legal nature are tolerated outside of the jurisdiction of the Bar of which the lawyer is a member has always been most important for lawyers, especially those doing international legal work. The Committee on Comparative Procedure and Practice, Section of International Law of the American Bar Association has collected all regulations existing for foreign lawyers and published these regulations in 1977.[38] The legislation existing

36. Advocats d'Europe, Liège 1977, p. 199.
37. M. Michel Gaudet, 'Les Juristes d'Entreprise et la C.E.E.', Bulletin No. 3, October 1969, Association Belge des Juristes d'Entreprise.
38. 'Report on the Regulation of Foreign Lawyers', American Bar Association 1977.

already in many countries for the first time was complemented by a ruling which affects a number of states, namely the memberstates of the European Economic Communities. In a Council Directive of March 22, 1977 the Council of the European Communities adopted this directive 'to facilitate the effective exercise by lawyers of freedom to provide services'.[39] The memberstates have two years to adopt the national legislation required to carry this directive into effect and transform it into national law. Lawyers affected by the Directive are the members of the Bars of the various memberstates (including solicitors in the United Kingdom and Ireland). Each host memberstate is required to recognize lawyers who are admitted to practice in other memberstates and who render legal services in the host state. They are required to use the same professional titles used by them in the memberstate from which they come. In this directive, in article 6 lawyers in permanent employment (company lawyers) are expressly mentioned. Article 6 states that 'any memberstate may exclude lawyers who are in the salaried employment of a public or private undertaking from pursuing activities relating to the representation of that undertaking in legal proceedings insofar as lawyers established in that state are not permitted to pursue those activities'. By this article restrictions existing in the Federal Republic of Germany for Rechtsanwälte in permanent employment have been transferred into European law. On the other hand this article recognizes expressly the possibility of lawyers being in 'salaried employment of a private undertaking'. (Annex: English Wording of the Council Directive of March 22, 1977).

The European Community is also employer for a large number of jurists from all member countries. When we speak of company lawyers, the many jurists in public service are not covered by the definition of the position of the company lawyer. But it should not be forgotten that these jurists also have their problems and that they belong to the legal profession even if they work in a kind of professional 'diaspora'.[40]

39. Official Journal of the European Communities, No. L 78, 26 March 1977, pp. 17-18.
40. Dr. Jan Gijssels, 'De jurist in de internationale organisaties en in de bedrijven', Rechtskundig Weekblad 1970, pp. 1135-1140.

Annex:
Council Directive of 22 March 1977

to facilitate the effective exercise by lawyers of freedom to provide services (77/249/EEC)

THE COUNCIL OF THE EUROPEAN COMMUNITIES,

Having regard to the Treaty establishing the European Economic Community, and in particular Articles 57 and 66 thereof,

Having regard to the proposal from the Commission,

Having regard to the opinion of the European Parliament,

Having regard to the opinion of the Economic and Social Committee,

Whereas, pursuant to the Treaty, any restriction on the provision of services which is based on nationality or on conditions of residence has been prohibited since the end of the transitional period;

Whereas this Directive deals only with measures to facilitate the effective pursuit of the activities of lawyers by way of provision of services; whereas more detailed measures will be necessary to facilitate the effective exercise of the right of establishment;

Whereas if lawyers are to exercise effectively the freedom to provide services host Member States must recognize as lawyers those persons practising the profession in the various Member States;

Whereas, since this Directive solely concerns provision of services and does not contain provisions on the mutual recognition of diplomas, a person to whom the Directive applies must adopt the professional title used in the Member State in which he is established, hereinafter referred to as 'the Member State from which he comes',

HAS ADOPTED THIS DIRECTIVE:

Article 1

1. This Directive shall apply, within the limits and under the conditions laid down herein, to the activities of lawyers pursued by way of provision of services.

Notwithstanding anything contained in this Directive, Member States may reserve to prescribed categories of lawyers the preparation of formal documents for obtaining title to administer estates of deceased persons, and the drafting of formal documents creating or transferring interests in land.

2. 'Lawyer' means any person entitled to pursue his professional activities under one of the following designations:

Belgium:	Avocat – Advocaat
Denmark:	Advokat
Germany:	Rechtsanwalt
France:	Avocat
Ireland:	Barrister
	Solicitor
Italy:	Avvocato
Luxembourg:	Avocat-avoué
Netherlands:	Advocaat
United Kingdom:	Advocate
	Barrister
	Solicitor.

68

Article 2

Each Member State shall recognize as a lawyer for the purpose of pursuing the activities specified in Article 1 (1) any person listed in paragraph 2 of that Article.

Article 3

A person referred to in Article 1 shall adopt the professional title used in the Member State from which he comes, expressed in the language or one of the languages, of that State, with an indication of the professional organization by which he is authorized to practise or the court of law before which he is entitled to practise pursuant to the laws of that State.

Article 4

1. Activities relating to the representation of a client in legal proceedings or before public authorities shall be pursued in each host Member State under the conditions laid down for lawyers established in that State, with the exception of any conditions requiring residence, or registration with a professional organization, in that State.
2. A lawyer pursuing these activities shall observe the rules of professional conduct of the host Member State, without prejudice to his obligations in the Member State from which he comes.
3. When these activities are pursued in the United Kingdom, 'rules of professional conduct of the host Member State' means the rules of professional conduct applicable to solicitors, where such activities are not reserved for barristers and advocates. Otherwise the rules of professional conduct applicable to the latter shall apply. However, barristers from Ireland shall always be subject to the rules of professional conduct applicable in the United Kingdom to barristers and advocates.
When these activities are pursued in Ireland 'rules of professional conduct of the host Member State' means, in so far as they govern the oral presentation of a case in court, the rules of professional conduct applicable to barristers. In all other cases the rules of professional conduct applicable to solicitors shall apply. However, barristers and advocates from the United Kingdom shall always be subject to the rules of professional conduct applicable in Ireland to barristers.
4. A lawyer pursuing activities other than those referred to in paragraph 1 shall remain subject to the conditions and rules of professional conduct of the Member State from which he comes without prejudice to respect for the rules, whatever their source, which govern the profession in the host Member State, especially those concerning the incompatibility of the exercise of the activities of a lawyer with the exercise of other activities in that State, professional secrecy, relations with other lawyers, the prohibition on the same lawyer acting for parties with mutually conflicting interests, and publicity. The latter rules are applicable only if they are capable of being observed by a lawyer who is not established in the host Member State and to the extent to which their observance is objectively justified to ensure, in that State, the proper exercise of a lawyer's activities, the standing of the profession and respect for the rules concerning incompatibility.

Article 5

For the pursuit of activities relating to the representation of a client in legal proceedings, a Member State may require lawyers to whom Article 1 applies:
– to be introduced, in accordance with local rules or customs, to the presiding judge and, where appropriate, to the President of the relevant Bar in the host Member State;
– to work in conjunction with a lawyer who practises before the judicial authority in question and who would, where necessary, be answerable to that authority, or with an 'avoué' or 'procuratore' practising before it.

Article 6

Any Member State may exclude lawyers who are in the salaried employment of a public or private undertaking from pursuing activities relating to the representation of that undertaking in legal proceedings in so far as lawyers established in that State are not permitted to pursue those activities.

Article 7

1. The competent authority of the host Member State may request the person providing the services to establish his qualifications as a lawyer.
2. In the event of non-compliance with the obligations referred to in Article 4 and in force in the host Member State, the competent authority of the latter shall determine in accordance with its own rules and procedures the consequences of such non-compliance, and to this end may obtain any appropriate professional information concerning the person providing services. It shall notify the competent authority of the Member State from which the person comes of any decision taken. Such exchanges shall not affect the confidential nature of the information supplied.

Article 8

1. Member States shall bring into force the measures necessary to comply with this Directive within two years of its notification and shall forthwith inform the Commission thereof.
2. Member States shall communicate to the Commission the texts of the main provisions of national law which they adopt in the field covered by this Directive.

Article 9

This Directive is addressed to the Member States.

Done at Brussels, 22 March 1977.

V. Internal Organization of the Legal Department

A. The small Legal Department

The complexity of modern life and the fast growing number of laws and regulations make it indispensable for companies of small or moderate size to be informed and advised on legal questions. This legal service is normally performed by outside counsel. Very often, out of a close contact with outside counsel, it becomes necessary to have legal advice instantly available, and this is the beginning of a law department. It starts in general with one lawyer. This one man legal department usually attempts to handle only routine minor matters and to give general advice.[1] There are various estimates as to the number of employees in a company which justifies the employment of a 'resident' attorney. One estimate concludes that any manufacturer with 200 to 800 employees can support and should have a house counsel. This is admittedly a generality and the number of employees alone will not determine the size of the legal department. The determining factors are the type of business as well as the country in which the business operates.[2] But a reasonable estimate for a manufacturer in a highly industrialized (and therefore highly regulated) West European country is one attorney for each one thousand members of the workforce.

Once the executives of the company begin to appreciate the services being performed by a competent company attorney, their demands upon him will tend to increase, until he becomes so busy that he must hire assistants. The company law department is on its way to expansion.

The small legal department, which thus normally grows out of the employment of one company lawyer[3] should be able to perform about all the legal services of the company except legal specialities and matters of very great importance. All of its members have to be good all-round lawyers, who can step in and substitute for one another in any type of legal business coming up. Most of its members must necessarily be experienced lawyers in order

1. David S. Ruder: 'A Suggestion for Increased Use of Corporate Law Departments in Modern Corporations', The Business Lawyer January 1968, pp. 341-363.
2. Robert R. Hyatt: 'Of House Counsel', Practical Lawyer, May 1957, pp. 72-81.
3. Lawrence S. Apsey: 'Organization of a Corporate Legal Department', The Business Lawyer, July 1959, pp. 944-956.

to cope with the many day-to-day routine problems coming up in a small corporation. Very seldom will this type of legal department have the opportunity and time for specialization. The small legal department has the advantage of being able to operate very compactly. It is possible to keep all members informed about all, or at least most important, matters going on and handled by the department. The size of the company and the legal department brings about a very close relationship between the management of the company and the staff of the legal department. Personal contacts tend to be easy and frequent. Organization and operation of law departments in smaller companies are less formal and standardized than in large companies. They have different problems and management frequently is less systematic and less bureaucratic.[4]

B. The large Legal Department

It is in the large legal department where organizational problems come into the open. But I would like to add immediately that the organizational problems of the large legal department are in most cases, merely a reflection of the organization of the company itself and its problems. The organization of the legal department cannot be seen per se; it must be adjusted to the company organization in order to be effective in its service.

This correlation between company organization and legal department organization became obvious when, after World War II large companies, first in the United States and afterwards in the rest of the world, decentralized. Autonomous commercial divisions with a more or less autonomous management can be found today even in smaller companies. Company decisions on major business matters have been delegated in these organizations to divisional management. Correspondingly, many companies also decentralized their company legal department, at least to a certain extent, and legal responsibility was delegated to divisional counsels.

1. Division Counsel

The decentralization of legal work creates a number of problems but it has also advantages.

aa. First the advantages of the decentralization of legal work which follows the division principle: The divisional counsel is in very close contact with the business he is working for. He has a close personal rapport with the management of the division and he is familiar with its business, its products, its needs, its problems and its personnel.[5] Sometimes the divisions are not housed in

4. Quintin Johnstone and Dan Hopson jr.: op. cit., pp. 236-237.
5. Joseph R. Creighton: 'Corporate Law Departments adjust to Corporate Decentralization', The Business Lawyer, July 1961, pp. 1004-1013.

one place, but they are (especially in the United States), spread over a large geographical area. A centralized legal department is, naturally not as familiar with the division problems as a division counsel who is on the spot. He saves time by being on the spot. His contact with the responsible personnel is much better and business problems can be solved faster and more efficiently. He knows better which priorities are to be established.

The advantage of the division lawyer is that often he will know the facts in advance and has better access to the facts. He knows background matters, historical factors, business relationships and personalities. This gives him the possibility to solve problems fast and sometimes, or usually without the long research, that only would delay the decision-making process.

The division counsel, therefore, can be an asset to the company and the division. He is readily available and in many cases can help faster than a centralized legal department could, even discounting the long distances between the division and the centralized legal department. This justifies a miniature legal department for the decentralized division. It is only logical that in such cases a division counsel is responsible for all, or almost all, of the legal needs of the division. His contact with the client is permanent, and after some time he will very likely be involved in the day-to-day decision-making process of the division, thus saving valuable time.

Other companies have organized on the basis of one central legal department and branch law departments located in large cities.

The law department of Shell Oil Company in the United States, which is termed by Johnstone and Hopson as 'one of the best in the United States'[6] has a home office staff in New York and field law offices in Los Angeles, Denver, Houston, Midland (Texas) and New Orleans. This decentralization is necessitated by the exploration and production facilities of the company. The geographical divisionalization brings about coordination problems for the 83 lawyers (in 1964) involved.

bb. The decentralization or divisionalization also has disadvantages. The division counsel normally cannot specialize in a certain legal field. He tends to be involved more deeply in the normal course of business and sometimes not only in legal work, but also in administrative or commercial work. This takes much of his time and keeps him away from the legal work he is supposed to do. It increases the tendency for him to identify himself with business objectives. He thus is in danger of losing his objectivity. His field of legal activity is necessarily relatively narrow because he is not normally exposed to new ideas coming from other clientele.

Very often the division counsel does not have competent professional supervision. He will normally be a one-man-organization, and therefore, he does not have the chance to discuss difficult legal problems with his colleagues. It is very likely that he also will not be able to follow pending legislation: a

6. Quintin Johnstone and Dan Hopson jr.: op. cit., p. 211.

73

point which is essential for any company counsel, because this might enable the division to decide in time on measures and ways which might be of considerable advantage for the future.

There is another important point which I would like to stress: his professional independence as a lawyer can be endangered by the fact that his superiors are not doing legal work. They are managers. Consequently, they tend to think in strict hierarchical structures and treat the division lawyer like all other subordinates who have to follow instructions as all other members of the division. This might result in conflicts concerning professional ethics.

He must be careful not to become a prisoner of management. An additional factor which might reduce the professional independence of a division counsel can be his desire to move into a management position. Such promotions are frequent. The company lawyer who is doing legal work should realize that he has been employed by the company as lawyer and not as future manager. If he has the desire to go into management because his interest is stronger in business than in law then it would be better not to hire him because he will never be able to achieve the distance from the business which is necessary to become an independent legal adviser.[7]

cc. Large companies today have affiliates in foreign countries. Many of these companies are so big that they require their own legal departments. National lawyers in affiliates are required because of the different legal systems prevailing in various countries, for instance in Europe. Here also the problems of coordinating the central legal department with the work of the company lawyers in the affiliated companies exist.

The problem exists especially for large transnational companies which have in practically each European country a separate affiliated company. Some American companies have tried to solve the existing coordination problem between the centralized legal department in the United States of America and the company legal departments in various European countries by creating a coordinating European legal department. The General Counsel of this department resides in a European country and coordinates from there the company lawyers in the European affiliates.

He reports either directly to the US legal department or to the President of the international division. Frequently a European lawyer is appointed as General Counsel of the European liaison legal department because his legal training enables him to better understand the different legal systems in Europe. This coordination has become especially important in view of the extensive legislation of the common market authorities. This legislation applies not only to the affiliated companies working in Europe but also influences the legal situation of the parent company in the United States of America. On the other hand American antitrust legislation applies not only to the territory of the United States of America, but also to the affiliates of

7. David S. Ruder: op. cit., p. 352.

US-companies overseas. Therefore, a European coordinating legal department can be of considerable assistance to the General Counsel of the parent company in the United States, and it also has certain advantages for the company lawyers working in the affiliated companies in Europe (Chart I).

Chart I

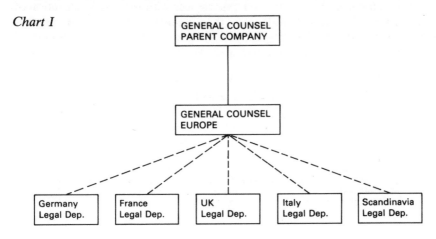

dd. Which organizational structures are available to solve the difficulties resulting from the divisionalization of the legal work in an enterprise?
One possible solution is that the General Counsel controls the professional quality of the work of the division counsel or the counsel of the affiliated company, but that these counsels report in all other respects to the general manager of the division or the head of the division of the affiliated company.

The division lawyer or the lawyer of the affiliated company is responsible in some respects to the company's chief lawyer, but he also owes responsibility to the division manager of the head of the affiliated company. In other words he has two masters. Creighton points out[8] that this duality of obligation is also existing in large law firms, and can be solved only with considerable goodwill on both sides. The dual relationship must not induce the divisional lawyer to report matters of importance to the General Counsel if such reports bypass the division manager. The proper channel for the reporting of divisional problems, even if legal problems are involved is from divisional management to company management and not from division counsel to General Counsel (Chart II). In other companies division lawyers are almost autonomous and look to the General Counsel only for advice and consultation. Such structures are partly historical, partly due to the development of the organization or due to personalities. This type of organization neglects the fact that the company rather than the division, is the responsible unit in matters of law. Many of the legal matters that arise in the division are really company

8. Joseph R. Creighton, op. cit., p. 1008.

problems. Their handling can have significant implications for the company as a whole. Therefore, no matter where legal problems arise in the company, they have to move very quickly into the company management and the company legal staff.[9]

Only few companies have had good experiences with the divisionalization of legal advice. It requires more lawyers than a central legal department. It is difficult to coordinate the different lawyers giving advice on the same legal subject and, as has been mentioned already, it is difficult for the lawyers to

Chart II

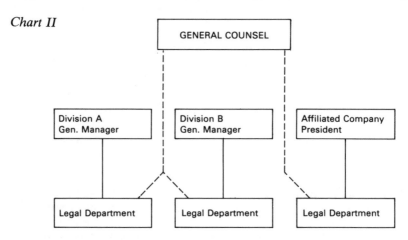

maintain their independence and objectivity. Therefore, this type of divisionalized legal department is advisable only for companies with very large divisions or affiliated companies in different countries.[10] An additional problem is the supervision and judgement on the quality of the work done. The division counsel or the lawyer in the affiliated company must be acceptable to the manager of the organizational unit. His personal relationship with this management must be good, otherwise cooperation cannot be expected. The lawyer must also be effective. The effectiveness can best be judged by the local management. The General Counsel is far away and it is very difficult for him to judge the effectiveness of the lawyer in the division or the affiliated company. He has a general overview but it is difficult for him to decide in detail whether the work done has been done properly under the existing circumstances.

Therefore, a good relationship must exist between the General Counsel and the members of the central legal department on one side and between the management of the division or the affiliated company on the other side. Contact between the company lawyer and his central legal department should

9. National Industrial Conference Board, 'Top Management Organization in Divisionalized Companies', Studies in Personnal Policy Nr. 195 (1965), pp. 63-67.
10. Arthur C. O'Meara: 'Organizational Structure, Operation and Administration of a large Corporate Law Department (25 or more lawyers)', The Business Lawyer April 1962, pp. 584-594.

be furthered if distance permits this. Regular meetings of all members of the central legal department with the members of divisional legal departments or affiliated legal departments are valuable. Such conferences must be prepared very carefully. They should deal primarily with subjects which are of interest to the entire company. In addition, they can be used to inform the 'outposts' about legal developments affecting the company and, therefore, influencing their work.

Such conferences not only strengthen the personal relations between the lawyers who work in remote areas and their colleagues in the central department, but they are part of an educational process which is necessary to make sure that all lawyers working for the company have the same information and the same background. Close connections will support the effectiveness of the work done on both sides. Whatever the organization chart shows, it must be ascertained that all legal advice given to the managers of the company, regardless of where they are, is the same. Different members of the legal department cannot give different advice to management. This results in a loss of confidence in the company legal department.

2. Central Legal Department

The opposite principle to decentralized legal advice is the centralized legal department which, because of its size, can train legal specialists with a high degree of knowledge. These departments function quite similarly to large law firms with specialists in those fields of law which are of particular importance to the company. The work of the individual lawyer can be supervised and closely followed by the head of the department or the General Counsel. A department with this organization has a manageable structure.

If the legal department employs a greater number of attorneys it is recommendable to include a supervisory level between the General Counsel and the various divisions, branches, Dezernate, sections or how the substructures might be called in the country concerned. There can be, for example, two Assistant General Counsels with one half of the division heads reporting to one and the other half to the other Assistant General Counsel. It should be considered very carefully whether or not such an organizational structure within the legal department is advisable but it must be ensured that the General Counsel is kept informed of all important matters dealt with by the department so that he will be able to give proper information to his colleagues in the top company management.

C. Specialization

The complexity of law and the increasing volume of legislation and regulations require specialization. Therefore, the future for the work of the company lawyer (outside counsel as well as house counsel), belongs to the specialist. He has to be skilled and broadly experienced in his specialized field of law. This statement was already made some twenty years ago and it is today even more valid than at that time.[11] Specialization increases efficiency and enables a lawyer to do more work in less time. The experienced specialist is certain of the accuracy and completeness of his work. The specialist can more easily build a reputation, not only among his colleagues in other companies and through work in trade associations, but also in his own company and its management. Obviously, the specialization in a particular field of law is justified only if the volume of problems in that field of law requires such special knowledge. The fields of law for which specialization seems advisable depend on the activities of the company. Many companies have frequent problems with antitrust law, unfair competition regulations, laws of the EEC, trademark laws or similar fields. Others are more concerned with more remote legal activities such as maritime and transportation law. Therefore, the activity of the company inevitably prescribes the necessity for specialization in subject matters or fields of law. The number of fields of law will be determined by the size of the department and the frequency of the legal problems that arise. A specialization is not justified unless the volume of problems in this area of law requires the full time of the larger part of a lawyer's time (Chart III).

Chart III   SPECIALIZED DEPARTMENT

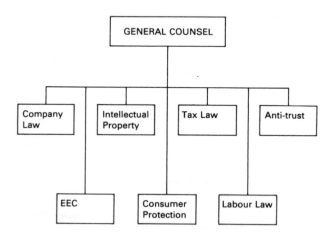

This Chart shows only some examples for specialized sections in the Legal Department

11. Leon Hickman: 'Corporate Counsel and the Bar', The Business Lawyer, July 1957, pp. 925-943. Louis Deymas points out that the company lawyer can be specialized in only a few legal fields, those in which his company is active. In all other fields he acts more as a legal contact who identifies the legal problems which warrant closer studies by a specialist ('Le Service
→

And now for illustration some areas of specialization:

aa. Of great importance for many industrial companies are patent and trademark problems. There are differences of opinion as to whether the patent section should be part of the legal department. Patent sections are sometimes independent, sometimes attached to the research department and sometimes incorporated in the legal department. The work of the patent department is primarily of a legal nature, since patents and their enforcement depend on legal decisions in the patent office and in the courts. The prosecution of patent applications, though, is a speciality which requires a technical education. In this field the patent section should work independently although it is part of the legal department. However, close liaison is necessary in many other fields especially review and negotiation of patent license agreements, non-infringement warranties, secret technical information, etc. The close correlation between patents and trade secrets is one major reason why patent work should be handled in an organizational unit which is part of the legal department. The background of information which is available to the attorney in the legal department permits him to develop procedures which accomplish the legal protection desired in a very complicated field of law.[12] The situation for trademarks and other industrial property rights is similarly more legalistic than before. These areas have become even more legalized by the effect of the antitrust laws and the extensive rulings of the Common Market Authorities on patents, trademarks and their use, including licences.

The patent policy is a company matter and cannot be confined to the patent section or the legal department. The development of such a policy requires the combined knowledge and judgement of representatives of research, sales, patents and law. Therefore a patent committee having competence for the entire company frequently determines what use the company will make of patents.[13] A patent committee combines the necessary expertise with the skill of the legal department and thus potential legal problems which could develop from research actions can be solved in advance for the benefit of the company.[14]

bb. An area of organizational conflict can be the tax law. Some companies have attached the tax division to financial departments. Considering that the tax law is part of the general field of law and that many general legal terms are applicable to tax law, it certainly is more efficient to have the head of the

---

Juridique dans une Entreprise Industrielle et Commerciale ce que l'on Attend de Lui, et L'"Equilibre Mental" qu'il droit acquerier pour y Repondre', Le Juriste d'Entreprise, pp. 253-259).
12. Charles S. Maddock: 'The Corporation Law Department', Harvard Business Review March-April 1952, pp. 119-136.
13. Lawrence S. Apsey: op. cit., pp. 944-956.
14. Leonard P. Prusak: 'The Lawyer's Role in Industrial Management', The Business Lawyer July 1962, pp. 1033-1043.

tax division report to the General Counsel of the company. Another solution is that the tax division of the legal department does not serve as the responsible tax agency, the organization which does the formal tax reporting and deals with the formalities of taxation. But the legal department should act as legal adviser to the responsible department which in such cases, would be under the jurisdiction of the comptroller or the financial vice president.[15]

cc. An important field of law in most countries is antitrust. Fast changing legislation, which is implemented by court decisions, requires the specialization of at least one lawyer in a larger legal department. Spectacular antitrust and cartel cases in various countries have shown the importance of counselling, especially middle management, on antitrust or cartel legislation.[16] Especially in this field the practice of preventive law is most important and the company lawyer has a very responsible educational function in these fields of law. Therefore, it is necessary for every member of the legal department to have a working knowledge of cartel law, and in larger companies at least one specialist must be able to interpret to his colleagues the developments in this field of law.

dd. During the last twenty years a completely new field of law has developed in Europe in the Common Market. The European Economic Community and its institutions have promulgated regulations and rules under the Treaty of Rome which govern large parts of the European industry but also the industry of foreign countries operating in the Common Market. Regulations require notification of the commission for certain agreements and business practices. A lawyer of supranational legislation and regulations has spread over the national laws of the member countries and company lawyers especially have had to become experts in this new field of legislation. This has made the job of the company lawyer far more complex in our time than at any time before.[17] Also in this case every member of the company legal department must have a working knowledge of these regulations: in addition, specialization and participation in the discussion of new regulations as happens frequently in the legal committees of trade associations etc. is essential for the legal department, as well as for the company. There are many cases now in which decisions of the commission of the ECC or the European High Court in Luxemburg have deeply affected companies or industries; therefore, this field requires the permanent attention of a well organized legal department.

ee. Also in most other legal fields the past 25 years have brought a tremendous change in legislation. This can be stated for practically all specialized legisla-

15. Arthur C. O'Meara, op. cit., p. 586.
16. Joseph R. Creighton: 'Corporate Counsel and Antitrust', American Bar Association Journal July 1962, pp. 654-656.
17. Sylvester C. Smith, jr.: 'The Outlook of Corporate Counsel', The Business Lawyer January 1963, pp. 323-336.

tions.[18] The prospering world economy of the post World War II industrial period has shown defects and shortcomings in the relation between industry and the public. Consequently, parliaments and governments have regulated large areas sometimes to protect consumers, sometimes to strengthen the state influence. Hence, legal departments of companies had to cope with these new developments and in some countries, including the Federal Republic of Germany, complete new bodies of law have been created for certain types of industry which never existed before and which require not only the attention of the legal department in fulfilling the requirements of these laws, but also a permanent contact with the authorities charged with supervising these laws in order to explain the necessities of industry and the feasibility of compliance. A cooperation between the legal department and the public relations department of a company can be very helpful in these matters.[19]

Specialization should not start too early. Young lawyers must first gather a broad basic experience under adequate supervision and control before specializing in some particular field of law. Mobility can be achieved by rotating the young lawyer between several units in the legal department before he is trained in a particular speciality. Only a good generalist can later become a good specialist. This is important not only for the lawyer himself but also for the department. Within the department it frequently becomes necessary to change jobs. Therefore, a specialist should not be so far away from the basic work that he is no longer able either to do basic work or to change his special field of law.

The training and education of a company lawyer never ceases. He often has the opportunity to participate in various management schools, to take particular courses at law schools so as to develop educational efficiency in a particular legal speciality, and to attend bar association meetings and various other conferences dealing with specialized fields of law. All such activities better equip him to practise his profession and thus to serve his company.

D. The Coordination within the Legal Department

A legal department with specialized attorneys creates problems of coordination. In all cases, where more than one specialist is involved they must work together. The General Counsel has to make sure that a close cooperation exists among the specialists. There are various means to achieve this. One possibility is to place the responsibility for such a case with one person and see to it that there is a coordination between the specialists involved.

Specialization has, unfortunately, the tendency to alienate the specialist from

18. Sylvester C. Smith, jr.: 'The Changing Status of Corporate Counsel', New York State Bar Journal, February 1963, pp. 9-20.
19. John W. Hill: 'Corporation Lawyers and Public Relations Counsel', The Business Lawyer April 1959, pp. 587-608.

the businessman. Businessmen usually prefer to have a close contact with one member of the legal department and it is very difficult for them to decide which specialist to contact in a particular case. It is also extremely important for the specialist to maintain close contact with middle management in the company. From experience we all know that the necessity for legal counsel is greatest on the middle management level.[20] For these reasons the ideal law department organization has to combine legal specialities with an organizational structure allowing a close personal relationship with management. To achieve this it has proven very successful to have certain divisions or subsidiary companies assigned to one contact lawyer in the law department. This lawyer keeps close contact with these organizational units and knows his clients and their problems which can be very specific for the products produced and/or distributed in this organizational unit. He knows the environment in which this unit has to work. He is the legal counsel of this division and/or organizational unit and he knows how to handle the many problems that come up in the daily business of this unit[21] (Chart IV).

Chart IV

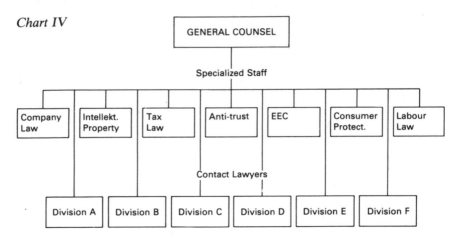

One disadvantage of this solution is that these contact lawyers seldom can specialize in certain fields of law because the very close contact with their organizational unit makes it almost impossible to specialize. Therefore, it is necessary to find a combination and a good working relationship between the contact lawyer and the specialist. This is difficult to coordinate, but the organizational pattern can be established in such a way that the contact lawyer brings the work from the client. He collects the facts and the specialist finds the solution. This probably sounds more complicated than it is, and its functioning will be dependent on the size of the company, the size of the legal

---

20. David S. Ruder: op. cit., p. 355.
21. National Industrial Conference Board, Studies in Business Policy, no. 39, 'Corporate Legal Department', 17, 1950, p. 6.

82

department and the geographical situation. If a number of divisions are located in one geographical area, this system works better than in a highly decentralized company where divisions or affiliated companies are located over large areas.

Also combinations of these systems can be practical (Chart V). It should be emphasized again that the organization of the legal department will always have to reflect the organization of its client – the company. If a company has a complicated organization the legal department will have to adjust to it. Special forms of organization in companies require a counter part in the legal department because the legal department is a service unit and it has to provide excellent legal service for its clients: it must be organized to solve all questions coming up. In order to do this in a most efficient way, its organization must be suited to the necessities of the corporation of which it is only a part.

As in all other departments in large companies the legal department also has an authority structure. The control pattern is like a pyramid: one lawyer is at the top. The General Counsel has great power, but also great responsibility. The personality of the General Counsel influences the entire department. He can knit the organization together and create a basic loyalty to the company. This is especially important for junior lawyers who should have easily access to the General Counsel and others at the top of the organizational structure. Personal association and close collegial ties among lawyers in the department, regardless of their rank in the company, will result in efficient work and company loyalty. This relationship is more difficult to achieve, but even more important for lawyers working in field law offices or legal departments of affiliated companies. Frequent personal contacts will help to solve coordination problems hopefully before they arise. Most important is a steady interchange of information and knowledge between individual members at all levels. Discussions between seniors and juniors must take place without loss of face. 'Every member of the department must accept that tomorrow someone may be away and that he then has to deal with a subject he knows little or nothing about. Or that a major operation may start which involves a number of attorneys, leaving the remainder to cope with everything else. So the organization must be flexible in the extreme – pooling of knowledge, pooling of information, not hesitating to go to someone-senior or not'.[22]

E. Organization Charts and Departmental Job Description

Functional and specialized legal departments should draw organization charts showing the responsibilities and specialization for each lawyer in the department. The advantage of such charts is the definition of responsibility for each section of the department. In addition, the personnel of the company can use

22. F.U.J. O'Brien, 'The Law Department of an Oil Company in London', The Business Lawyer November 1960, pp. 113-123.

Chart V

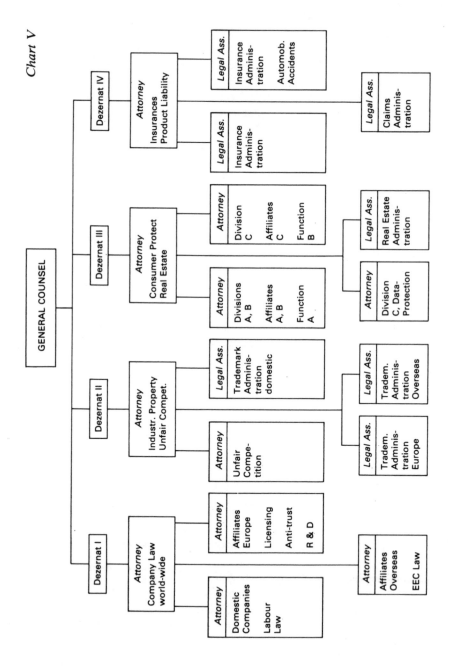

84

these charts to find out which contact lawyer or specialist they have to call upon in each case. To achieve this purpose and to make the chart understandable for non-lawyers, in other words for the clients of the legal department, it is necessary to have the charts as simple as possible. Lawyers have a tendency to be too explicit in the definition of competences (at least in certain countries). If this explicitness or exaggerated explicitness is used to draw the organization chart it will not be very helpful for the personnel of the company. In addition to being a working paper for the legal department the organization chart has a kind of public relations effect. It makes the internal distribution of work between the sections within the legal department transparent for the clients. If one looks at it under these aspects it has an important function and, therefore, deserves the attention of all members of the department. The entire staff must try to word it as 'unlegal' as possible without endangering its character as a valuable tool for making contacts with all management levels of the company.

The departmental job description describes the work of the legal department and especially the contacts with other departments which sometimes do semi-legal work. This could be tax work or personnel administration, patent work and similar activities. Also the departmental job description defines the authority of the legal department and the sole responsibility for certain kinds of work.

While the organization chart is the internal work rule the departmental job description states the position of the legal department within the entire company. Therefore, both papers have some inter-relationship and build the definition and structure for the organization of the department.

The attached example for a departmental job description tries to serve as a model but it must be kept in mind that of course the situation will be different in each company.

Annex:
Job Description of the Legal Department

1. The Legal Department manages or performs all legal matters of the enterprise. This includes formal legal relations among the enterprise, its shareholders and the various supervisory boards. The Department renders consultative services on all legal questions and advises appropriate parties within the enterprise whenever new or proposed legislation, government regulations or court decisions may materially affect the Company. It is in charge of litigation except as otherwise set forth below.

2. The Legal Department handles all activities in the field of company law such as incorporations, dissolutions, joint ventures, mergers, acquisitions and liquidations. It takes part in negotiations of such activities, prepares the draft contracts and prepares the documentation for contracts. It prepares the meetings of the shareholders and of other bodies and draws up the Minutes. It administers all relevant documents in the field of company law.
It watches and evaluates the legal structure of the enterprise and consults the various management, supervisory and advisory bodies with respect to the possible legal structures and the legal consequences.

3. The Legal Department handles all registrations in the Commercial Register as well as all necessary notifications and publications.

4. The Legal Department administers all company shells of the enterprise.

5. The Legal Department prepares the orders of procedure by and for the management; supervisory and advisory bodies of the enterprise, including its affiliated companies.

6. The Legal Department prepares drafts of standard and individual contracts of every kind. Its members take part in negotiations on contracts. Draft contracts prepared by third parties are forwarded to the Legal Department for legal clearance before they are concluded. It is in charge of the interpretation of contracts.

7. The Legal Department prepares the General Conditions of Sale of the enterprise and adjusts them as may be necessary because of legal developments from time to time.

8. The Legal Department deals with all judicial enforcements of unpaid accounts receivable and handles executions as well as settlements and insolvencies.

9. The Legal Department advises the Personnel Department in all matters concerning personnel and industrial relations laws and regulations. It handles the necessary litigation in this field. It prepares standard employment and pension contracts as well as Memoranda and Articles of Association and agreements with respect to pension schemes.

10. The Legal Department handles all notifications, applications, information and legal matters which are required by the cartel and antitrust agencies of those countries or communities in which the enterprise is doing business. It follows the legislation, government regulations and court decisions in this field and examines all activities of the enterprise with respect to the applicable trade regulation and antitrust laws.

11. The Legal Department advises in all matters involving administrative and regulatory agencies as far as such matters relate to the application and interpretation of laws and regulations (e.g. Zoning Regulations, Environmental Protection Laws, Production Permits).

12. At the request of the Finance Department, the Legal Department gives its opinion on tax questions and deals with such questions jointly with the Finance Department. The Legal Department files appeals and demurrers relating to tax purposes. The Finance Department and the Legal Department cooperate closely in carrying all appeals and demurrers to conclusion.

13. The Legal Department examines all advertising material, all statements in connection with advertising and all sales promotion material to assure their legality.

14. The Legal Department handles all registrations as well as the centralized documentation of all trademarks of all companies belonging to the enterprise and ensures the maintainance of the trademarks to the extent required by the enterprise. It examines own trademarks and trademarks of third parties as well as trademark applications in view of possible conflicts between registered owned trademarks and those of third parties. When necessary, it files appeals with the patent office or initiates legal procedures before the courts for decision of possible conflicts. It gives clearance for trademarks which the enterprise may use.

15. The Legal Department handles all litigation concerning disputes in the fields of patents and designs. Such litigation is handled in close cooperation with the Patent Department. All procedures aimed at the granting, nullification and cancellation of patents and designs are handled by the Patent Department.

16. The Legal Department examines and approves all licence and cooperation agreements before they are signed. All payments in connection with these agreements are dealt with by the Finance Department.

17. The Legal Department deals with and administers all consulting contracts.

18. The Legal Department deals with all insurance matters. It advises the enterprise and the affiliated companies on questions concerning insurance, and it purchases all insurance policies. It supervises and administers the insurance program and assures proper payment or collection of tariffs, premiums and rebates.
The Legal Department handles, in cooperation with the concerned parts of the enterprise, all insurance claims.
The Legal Department handles all communication with the insurance companies and the broker.

19. The Legal Department advises in and deals with all civil and criminal law matters concerning road traffic as well as all matters concerning accidents and liability.

20. The Legal Department handles all real estate transactions. It deals with acquisitions of real estate and obtaining of the necessary approvals of the competent bodies of the enterprise, and it is responsible for the proper registrations in the Land Registry. It prepares the reports containing the real estate owned by the enterprise. It administers all real estate of the enterprise as well as such real estate the administration of which has been assigned to it from time to time.

21. The Legal Department safeguards, within the framework of its responsibilities, the interests of the enterprise. It observes the pre-parliamentary and parliamentary procedure, the academic discussion and jurisdiction in the fields of its responsibility and reports on essential developments.

22. The Legal Department maintains on file all the company's documentation in the field of company law and all agreements.

VI. Administration

A. Legal Costs

No one realizes more than company lawyers how drastically the legal expenses of the company are rising. Not only are the rates of outside counsel going up from time to time as clerical and secretarial salaries, rents, supplies and other expenses increase, but the same is occuring in costs of travel, telephone charges and other items comprising disbursements on behalf of the company. At the same time new legislation and regulations are requiring companies, especially those which are regulated in more than one area or country, to utilize legal services more than ever. Other company expenses are also going up at a very rapid rate.

1. The Situation in the United States of America

The importance of the rise in legal bills is reflected drastically in publications which appear from time to time in American journals and newspapers. The New York Law Journal of December 20, 1976 reported that legal costs are up 300% and that, in addition to the sharp rise in legal costs, many companies are faced with more litigation than ever before. In the last fifteen years the number of cases filed in US Federal Trial Courts has nearly doubled. Similar increases can be noted in the State Courts. Certain categories of cases have risen even more dramatically.[1] Cases commenced in US Federal Courts have risen from 3,047 in 1956 to 102,400 in 1966 and to 171,617 in 1976.[2] According to the same source, civil right employment cases commenced in 1970 number-ed 344; in 1972, 1015; in 1974, 2472; and in 1976, 5321. Private antitrust cases commenced in 1970 totalled 877; in 1972, 1299; in 1974, 1230; and in 1976, 1504.

Costs of litigation have increased considerably and a day in court is estimated at $ 2,000 for a lawyer and $ 1,000 for transcripts. Modest amounts in litigation are too small for lawyers to handle because the costs of the proceedings bear

1. Tom Goldstein: 'A Dramatic Rise in Lawsuits and Costs Concerns Bar', New York Times May 18, 1977.
2. 'The Administrative Office of the United States Courts and Judicial Counsel of the Second Circuit', The New York Times May 18, 1977.

no reasonable relation to the matter in controversy. According to a recent estimate the average cost per hour for work done by outside counsel has risen to $79 compared with a cost per hour of $41 for work done by inside counsel. It is not surprising that under these circumstances the question of legal costs has drawn wide attention in the United States; however, similar experiences can also be seen in Europe. Ralph Nader, the well-known consumer advocate, claims that in 1975 the Singer Company paid its outside counsel $1,98 million in fees; Pennzoel $1,5 million, CBS $1,5 million and American Electric Power $1,45 million.[3] Some examples of enormous antitrust suits and the resulting costs were reported by Peter W. Bernstein in the article 'The Wall Street Lawyers are striving on Change'.[4] According to this report one New York law firm is working with 15 lawyers and 19 para-legals, defending Xerox in an antitrust action brought by SCM. The law firm working for SCM employed 12 lawyers on this case. The case began in 1973 and the trial opened on June 20, 1977. During this period SCM spent more than $10 million alone on this case. The company's president estimates that by the time the case goes to the jury costs will be close to $20 million. One of the largest Wall Street law firms representing IBM in an antitrust action brought by the government nine years ago has about 50% of the firm's manpower involved in this one case and IBM is paying a fee that has been estimated at $10 million per year for this case.

A second reason for increased legal costs are new areas of regulation which require additional legal attention and personnel. This development is not restricted to the United States of America, but can be observed in all industrialized countries. However, the United States of America is notable for being a society of laws: legislative bodies produce new laws at a very fast rate, more than 100,000 in some years. Federal agencies create an additional 35,000 or more new regulations every year.[5] American counsels point out that examples for additional work in new legal areas can be found especially in the Employees' Retirement Income Security Act (ERISA of 1974), The Occupational Safety and Health Act and The Toxic Substances Act. Increase in Consumer Legislation and the Legislation of Equal Opportunities are areas which company law departments are now concerned with.[6] Under these circumstances it is not surprising that in the United States the number of lawyers, compared with the population, is much higher than in any European country.

According to recent estimates, in 1977 there were 445,000 lawyers in the US

3. Ralph Nader and Mark Green: 'Don't Pay Those High Legal Bills', The New York Times Magazine, November 20, 1977.
4. Peter W. Bernstein: 'The Wall Street Lawyers are striving on Change', Fortune March 13, 1978, p. 104.
5. 'Those Lawyers', Time April 10, 1978, p. 50.
6. Ruth Hochberger: 'Do it yourself is Industry's Reply to Rising Legal Cost', New York Law Journal, December 20, 1976.

and by 1985 this number is to grow to 600,000.[7] In the US in 1954, there were 1492 lawyers per million people and by 1976 this number increased to 1920 lawyers per million.[8] It is interesting to compare some figures from other countries: Israel has 2,467 lawyers for every million inhabitants, Canada 703, the United Kingdom 588, the Federal Republic of Germany 449 and Japan 89. These figures indicate the increase in legislation and litigation in the US but also show that Japan, for instance, apparently lives less complicated; therefore, the number of lawyers per 1 million inhabitants is much lower than in any other highly industrialized country.

A committee of the New York State Bar Association estimated in 1974 that at that time 59,000 lawyers were practising in New York State – nearly double the number of all the solicitors and barristers in England. In view of the growing legal workload companies rapidly expand their in-house legal staff. Company law department practice is increasing at a faster rate than any other field of law practice. It is estimated that in the United States of America there are now between 35,000 and 40,000 lawyers practising in company law departments.

Tom Goldstein claims in the New York Times of November 20, 1977 that company lawyers now comprise the fastest growing segment of the legal profession, partly because they cost about half of what outside law firms charge for the same routine work. Exxon, for example, increased its company law department from 90 attorneys in 1965 to 119 in 1970 and to 195 in 1977. Mobil has more than 200 lawyers in its legal department and thus ranks in size with the biggest law firms in the United States.[9] J.C. Penny Company Inc. expanded its corporate legal department from 25 to 94 attorneys since 1965. The legal staff of Time Inc. has grown from 2 to 9 lawyers since 1960. New York Life Insurance Co. has 50 lawyers in its legal department.[10] Union Carbide increased its legal personnel from 92 in 1976 to 107 in 1978. At DuPont the number of legal personnel went up from 131 in 1973 to 153 in 1977.[11]

High costs and increased litigation sometimes result in unusual circumstances for the companies involved: Fortune[12] reported about an FTC case against the cereal industry. One of the defendants in this case, Quaker, hired in the course of this procedure the partner of the outside law firm who handled this antitrust case. This very unusual hiring of the outside counsel brought about some serious legal questions especially regarding conflict of interests. On the other hand it saved Quaker large amounts of fees for this litigation.

Under these circumstances it is not surprising that General Counsels control

7. Tom Goldstein: 'Job Prospects for Young Lawyers Dim as Fields Grows Overcrowded', The New York Times May 17, 1977.

8. 'Those Lawyers', Time April 10, 1978, p. 53.

9. Bernstein, Peter W., op. cit., p. 104.

10. Ruth Hochberger, op. cit.

11. W. David Gibson, op. cit., p. 34.

12. Walter Kiechel: 'The Soggy Case Against the Cereal Industry', Fortune April 10, 1978, p. 50.

the legal fees very strictly. Many General Counsels were once partners in large law firms and therefore know very well how large law firms calculate fees. They want to know as much as possible about the billing practices of the law firm which they employ.

Company lawyers make every effort to keep the company's legal expenses to an absolute minimum. It is necessary to think of steps that company lawyers can take to reduce the acceleration of fees by the elimination or modification of practices which, established in other days, are no longer appropriate as costs skyrocket. There are some savings which can be effectuated in law firms, but also in a company law department:

1.1. Duplication of effort in staffing must be avoided. If one lawyer can attent a meeting, handle a lawsuit or perform other services, one must avoid the use of two lawyers. Often it is necessary to have more than one lawyer in a matter, but this does not mean that lawyers must travel in twos or threes.

The Wall Street Journal of April 13, 1978 reported in an article on 'Costly Counsel' a remark made at an American Bar Association meeting: 'Attorneys, like nuns, travel in pairs or three at a time − with the clock running while the client watches helplessly'.

A memorandum as to what transpired at a meeting can often eliminate the need of a second or perhaps a third lawyer's presence. This refers to a practice of large law firms, where normally partners are always accompanied by associates (who do a substantial part of the work). This results in additional costs which can be avoided.

1.2. Another area in which one can economize is the assignment of the handling of a matter in the most economical manner insofar as the particular person or persons assigned to it are concerned. The objective must be to have the task competently performed at the lowest possible ultimate cost. In assigning a lawyer to handle a matter it must be born in mind how important and how complicated the matter is and whether a senior lawyer is required. If a younger lawyer with a lower hourly rate or income can perform the service, it should be assigned to this lawyer. Of course, it must be recognized that a specialist can sometimes perform a particular service more quickly than one with less experience or skill, so that even at a higher cost it can be more economical for the specialist to perform the service. The same applies to a lawyer who has previously handled an identical or similar matter.

Another consideration is whether the cost of supervision plus the cost of assigning a younger lawyer may not result in a higher total fee than would be incured were the senior lawyer to handle the matter himself.

These are but a few suggestions to help meet the company's growing concern over the size of its legal expenses. It is necessary to make every effort to keep these costs as low as possible. Unquestionably, these remarks apply to company law departments as well as outside counsel. More and more pressure must be exercised to economize in every possible way. In the United States of America a number of company law departments have established uniform systems for the preparation and submission of statements for fees and disbursements for the company. In other countries, like the Federal Republic of Germany, legislation exists regulating the fees of outside counsel. Other European countries operate under either of these two systems.

In general, regardless of the system that is being applied in the country, cost control has become a most important part of the activity of any company lawyer.

2. Allocation of Costs

It is very interesting to see how companies handle the allocation of costs resulting from the work of the legal department. A principle often used is to allocate the costs of a certain activity of the law department to the individual 'client' by directly charging time costs. Of course, there are other allocation keys possible, but the charge to the division that requested the help of the legal department reduces 'frivolous requests for legal aid'.[13]

One disadvantage of the direct allocation to the management unit, which has initiated the work of the legal department, is that management might refrain from consulting the law department in order to cut down costs, especially in cost conscious companies.

The Time Sheet

The system described is used very successfully by General Mills Inc., where the company's legal costs as a percentage of sales have declined for the last five years. Other companies use similar systems. In order to facilitate the computation of the costs to be charged, the attorneys in the department are organized as they would be in a regular law firm. They keep hourly-rate charge sheets, just as outside counsels do.[14] This record keeping provides for a breakdown of lawyer-time by general types of work for the total legal department. Professional services are also broken down by type of work. General Mills Inc. has broken down all expenditures (including corporate, centralized services and direct allocations) by percent for a given period of time as follows:

1. Patent   11,7%
2. Trademark   14,7%
3. Intellectual Property   3,9%
4. Government Regulations 15,5%

13. Ryan, John: 'Costly Counsel: Regulations, Fees Boost Companies' Legal Expenses', The Wall Street Journal April 13, 1978.
14. Ryan, John, op. cit.

5. Financial	8,2%
6. Speciality	10,6%
7. Contracts	21,8%
8. Consumer Matters	3,9%
9. Miscellaneous	9,7%

This breakdown indicates clearly the importance of the various legal activities in relation to the total work of the department. It also shows the burden of work regarding government regulations. Any system based on direct allocation must provide for a splitting of centralized service expenses to the 'client' divisions. At General Mills Inc. these principles have been described as follows:

'Actual expenses for outside professional services and other expense account items are recorded regularly, totaled for each division and allocated accordingly.

Lawyers' time logs are also totaled for each division and used as the basis for allocating the rest of the expenses, chiefly payroll, and travel. Both expenses for professional services and company lawyers are identified for allocation purposes by the activity receiving the service and the particular description of the work involved.

These actual totals are then projected separately for the year, with adjustment for known or expected variations between the actual recorded period and the balance of the year. The sum of the projected totals constitutes the allocation for a particular division.

Primary control over the centralized service allocations comes from the fact that such services are performed essentially at the request of the 'client' divisions. The division personnel is kept aware of both the expected costs and the realistic, probable or potential benefits, before the requested work is taken on. Thus, the 'program' is not considered as an authorization to spend up to the allocated amounts, but merely a best estimate of the cost of all services which will have been performed by mutual agreement during this period'.

The time utilized by each attorney is allocated to the division for which the work is done by using a work type code which breaks down in detail the categories of work as follows:

Work Type Codes

Patent (10)
11 US Patent Filing Evaluation
12 US Patent Applications
13 US Patent Operating Clearances
14 US Patent Policing Evaluation
15 US Patent or Know-How Licensing

21 Foreign Patent Filing Evaluation
22 Foreign Patent Applications
23 Foreign Patent Operating Clearances
24 Foreign Patent Policing Evaluation
25 Foreign Patent or Know-How Licensing
26 Foreign Patent Tax Maintenance

Trademarks (20)
31 US Trademark Searching & Clearance
32 US Trademark Applications
33 US Trademark Usage & Infringement Policing
34 US Trademark Licensing

41 Foreign Trademark Searching & Clearance
42 Foreign Trademark Applications
43 Foreign Trademark Usage & Infringement Policing
44 Foreign Trademark Licensing

Other Intellectual Property Law Matters (30)
45 Copyrights
46 Submitted Ideas
47 Employee Suggestion System
48 Publication Clearances
49 Disclosure & Secrecy Agreements

Government Regulations (40)
50 Federal Trade Commission
51 Food & Drug Administration
52 Consumer Product Safety Commission
53 Pending Legislation
54 Occupational Safety & Health Act
55 State Regulations
56 Discrimination Matters
57 Energy Matters
58 Ecological Matters
59 Other Governmental Regulations

Financial (50)
61 SEC
62 Financing
63 Financial (Misc. Treasurer)
64 Stock Transfer Matters
65 Stock Options & Executive Incentive Plan
66 Benefit Plans − Pension, VIP & TSP
67 Benefit Plans − Insurance

68 Benefit Plans – Other
69 Corporate Matters (Organization, Minutes, etc.)

Specialty (60)
71 Packaging & Advertising Review
72 Antitrust
73 Labor Relations
74 Personnel Matters
75 Bankruptcy Matters
76 Tax
77 Insurance Matters
78 Legal Research – Special Projects

Contracts (70)
81 Contracts (all other)
82 Performance Contracts (Charge Division)
83 Acquisition & Dispositions (Drafting, etc.)
84 Real Estate Matters
85 Computer Contracts

Consumer Matters (80)
90 Consumer Complaints
91 Community Affairs

Miscellaneous (99)
94 Seminars, Meetings, Readings (Charge 700)
95 Staff Meetings (Charge 700)
96 General & Administrative
97 Vacations Only (Charge 700)
98 Paid Time Off (Sick Time, Holidays, etc.) (Charge 700)

Correspondingly, a Division Allocation Code permits the exact allocation not only to divisions but also to individual management organizations of each division.
The attorney working on a project allocates his working time by entering the appropriate codes into a time sheet (see attached form).

Law Department Time Utilization

Time Allocation
ATTORNEY NAME _____ (1-8)

TRANS, CODE _____ ATTORNEY NO. _____ MONTH _____ DATE _____
                        (9-11)   (22-23)

                                        TOTAL HOURS _____

DIV ALLOC 12-15	WORK TYPE 16-19	LIT 20	YR 21	HOURS 24-28	+ −	WEEK 1	WEEK 2	WEEK 3	WEEK 4	WEEK 5	NOTES
0	00		1								
0	00		1								
0	00		1								
0	00		1								
0	00		1								
0	00		1								
0	00		1								
0	00		1								
0	00		1								
0	00		1								
0	00		1								
0	00		1								
0	00		1								
0	00		1								
0	00		1								

97

Allocation Keys

Another method of distributing the costs of the legal department is the use of certain allocation keys for the entire company. One key often used is the turnover of each department or division in relation to the toal company turnover.

An unwanted result of this system can be that divisions with high turnover, but few legal problems, have to bear a proportionally higher share of the entire legal costs than would be justified by the legal work required by this division. It is very difficult to find the right way to distribute the costs; and this problem affects not only the law department, but also all other staff departments which are not profit centres, but cost centers. Cost centers necessarily must be financed by the profit centers and management has to decide in which way each profit center contributes to the expenses of the cost centers. This burden must be born jointly by all profit centers.

On the other hand, cost centers have to economize as much as possible – as profit centers too – in order to make the entire company profitable.

Therefore, the question of financing the legal department should be seen from the aspect of the use and benefit the entire company will have from a well operating law department. The financial departments have to decide how the costs are to be distributed. This, of course, will be depedent upon the general principles which are in effect for the entire company.

B. Non-Legal Personnel

1. Legal Assistant

One method to reduce the costs is the use of legal assistants or para-legal personnel. This, of course, must be done carefully and with proper consideration to the length of time it would take a legal assistant to perform the task compared with the time a lawyer would require. However, there are many services which the legal assistant, especially when he or she has developed an expertise in certain areas, can perform at least as well as a lawyer and at substantially lower costs, always, of course, subject to lawyer review when a legal matter is involved.

In Anglo-Saxon countries the legal assistant or legal executive has a long standing history. Legal executives in England are a separate profession. They qualify by taking examinations, which have the same degree of difficulty as the examination which a solicitor has to take, but these examinations cover only a special field of law. In these specialized fields of law legal executives have the same degree of competence as a solicitor but they always work under supervision of a solicitor. English law clerks are highly skilled and have a respected status in the legal profession. They enjoy a great deal of autonomy and independence.

Also in Canada and in the United States the law clerk played an important role and clerkship was sometimes part of the education for lawyer. Due to the post-war-boom and the acute shortage of manpower in the legal profession, the para-legal, or law clerk as we know him today, emerged.

The US and Canadian codes of professional responsibility for lawyers recognize that a lawyer can delegate to clerks, secretaries, and other lay-persons such matters as can be performed under the law and which are not in violation of the 'unauthorized practice of law' statutes existing in many countries. Many law departments and law firms have found that through training and experience non-legal personnel can perform functions previously performed by lawyers.

In large US law firms so-called 'executive assistants', 'legal assistants', 'para-legals', 'para-professionals' − each firm has its own term for this profession − have taken over part of the work. Paul Hoffman reports in his book 'Lions in the Street'[15] that many lawyers refer to them as 'para-troops'. These legal assistants come from college, and their function is different in each law department and law firm. Basically they do much of the non-legal work which would be otherwise done by young lawyers. The organizations for para-legal personnel require of potential members that they have either worked as a para-legal for a certain number of years or have attended a para-legal training program.

There are wide fields of use for legal assistants in company law departments: they can prepare law suits for the attorney, assist him in the search for proper literature and be his personal aide in many legal matters; but most important is the independent work they can do, for instance in the insurance field, automobile accident cases, trademark matters and similar activities. In these fields legal assistants can do most of the work independently if they have the proper training. Probate work, corporate law, litigation and real estate are other fields of activity for legal assistants.

The corporate law assistant keeps the minute-books, stock record-books, corporate seals and other corporate documents. He sees to it that all formalities are carefully taken care of and that company records are complete. In some countries, he or she can also handle the filing of applications with the company register. All this is done under the supervision of an attorney.

Equally valuable is the activity of a real estate assistant. The real estate department has to do a lot of formal legal work which can be done easily by a trained expert in this field even if he does not have a lawyers training. Examination of title, the use of public records and registrations with the landregister, and other formalities, as well as mortgage documents, calculation of real estate, taxes to be paid by the company and similar tasks are handled by him.

In the trademark area formal registration procedures, opposition to trademarks filed by other companies and all documentation connected therewith

15. Paul Hoffman: 'Lions in the Street', New York 1973, p. 132.

are handled by a trademark specialist without legal training.

In general, it can be stated that legal assistants are most helpful in company law departments if they have been properly trained. They are experts in their field and very frequently have more specialized knowledge about their field of activity than a lawyer could have. In addition, they help save costs and reduce the number of lawyers required. They make it possible for the lawyers to deal with purely legal matters and they relieve the attorneys of administrative work which is also an essential part of the activity of any legal department.[16]

2. Law Department Administrator

Company Law Departments and Law Firms require not only competent lawyers but also administrators to run the administrative and management side of the department or firm. The recognition of the importance of a smooth functioning of the non-legal personnel brought about the profession of legal administrator or office manager. He or she is responsible for the office management and equipment and the effective work of the non-legal staff of the department. The Position Guide in a large American Legal Department describes the duties and responsibilities of the Legal Administrator as follows:

'Legal Administrator

I. Purpose

To plan, develop and implement administrative policies, procedures and control.

II. Accountabilities

1. Ensure effective personnel management for the law organization (including law department and secretary's office):
   a. Prepare required salary administration reports/surveys, and maintain law department personnel records.
   b. Ensure that adequate systems and methods of documentation and job descriptions exist and are current in all areas of the law organization.
   c. Perform periodic job evalution studies for department personnel.

16. 'Law Office Efficiency', A Collection of Presentations delivered at the American and Canadian Bar Associations' Economic and Management Conference, published 1972 by the American Bar Association and the Canadian Bar Association. The Joint Conference on Law Office Economics and Management was held in Toronto in June 1972. The book contains the speeches delivered at the conference. The topics dealt primarily with recruitement and training of legal assistants.

d. Develop and recommend organization of clerical activities within the law organization through selection, training and motivation of employees in clerical section to assure excellent current and future performance.

e. Provide substitution non-exempt help for the department and information desk and supervise the receptionist's activity.

2. Ensure effective financial management in assigned areas for the law organization:
   a. Prepare administrative budget and expense analyses for the secretary's office, patent law and general law departments. Prepare forecasts of department expense for corporate analysis.
   b. Prepare fiscal year forecasts for various divisions and subsidiaries, as requested, and prepare quarterly reports showing actual expense versus program.
   c. Supervise payment of all law department invoices and statements.
   d. Recommend and implement means for effective cost control within the department.

3. Ensure effective management in assigned areas for the law organization:

   a. Order office machines and furniture as needed and maintain control over equipment.
   b. Arrange office layout and handle rental charges.
   c. Coordinate with the Building Manager concerning proposed remodeling projects for the law department.
   d. Organize and approve vacation schedules for the secretary's office.
   e. Make appropriate arrangements for special department functions and parties.

4. Supervise the maintenance of records and schedules of trademarks and sales of new products and of products not in full scale marketing, for trademark purposes.
5. Check all distributions as calculated by the supervisor of stock programs for participants who retire or terminate their employment.
6. Attend and participate in Legal Administrators Association and seminars relating to defined accountabilities.

III. Relationships

This position reports to the General Counsel. The incumbent has broad contact with key executives staff groups and other employees throughout the organization.

IV. Dimensions

People:
Law Department Budget:

V. Job Specifications

Education: Bachelor Degree in Business Administration or equivalent.
Specialized or Technical Knowledge: Thorough knowledge of administrative and personnel practices.
Kind and Length of Experience: Incumbent should have a comprehensive familiarity with personnel and administrative problems and broad experience in management of personnel. Minimum of ten years experience.
Other Job Specifications (desirable, but not essential):
1. Degree in Accounting
2. Personnel Director or Administrator
3. Member of American Management Association
4. Member of Association of Legal Administrators'.[17]

This job description lists a great number of responsibilities which can be effectively performed by legal administrators and which relieve the attorneys of problems which should be handled by specialized personnel. The administrative head of the law department or law firm can perform most administrative and personnel matters much more effectively than a lawyer whose skills and abilities can be better used in legal work.

Law office administrators are normally the highest-paid non-professionals in the department or law office. They are vital to the smooth functioning of the office. These men and women have to run a complex business organization. To ensure their success and to avoid friction and problems a detailed job description is necessary.[18]

The Association of Legal Administrators is a US professional association whose membership is comprised of personnel who devote all of their time and efforts to the performance of managerial and administrative duties connected with a company's legal department, a private law firm, governmental, judicial or legal agency or other organization devoted primarily to the practice of law. The association had its first meeting in 1971 and numbers today more than 1,600 members in the United States and Canada. The stated purposes of the association are: to promote the exchange of experiences in the administration and management problem peculiar to legal organizations, to provide information on the value and availability of professional administrators, to improve the standards and qualifications for such administrators, to develop continuing education programs, and to participate in any other way in the advance-

17. Acknowledgement: The job description for Legal Administrator is published by courtesy of Clifford L. Whitehill, Vice-President and General Counsel, General Mills Inc.
18. Bruce D. Heintz: 'The Administrator in the Larger Firm', Legal Economics Summer 1978, pp. 31-33.

ment of the art of legal administration.[19]

Also in most European countries, this profession is well known and highly esteemed. In some countries, like the Fedral Republic of Germany, special rules exist for the training of non-legal personnel for law offices (and, of course, for legal departments).

Well-defined and well-working organizational structures in law departments and law firms save costs and increase the efficiency of the department. This was recognized in the United States of America at a very early stage, partly because law departments and law firms in this country are much larger in size than in Europe. It is, therefore, not surprising, that management consulting firms specialized for law firms and law departments exist and that they have investigated the specific organizational problems of legal organization.

C. Law Office Automation

On a worldwide scale the legal profession faces the problem of inflation with the increasing of costs of running law firms and legal departments, in particular personnel costs. At the same time the development of computers and new office machines has revolutionized the office organization Computers, computer-controlled typewriters, video terminals, microfilm and improved automated copy-duplicators speed and facilitate the fow of information in the legal office.[20]

This is not the place to describe at length the advantages of utilizing computer equipment for the law office. Experts who assist in computerizing trademarks, patents, real estate data, insurance programs, etc. are available in the business enterprise to which the law department belongs. Here the advantage of belonging to a large specialized organization is obvious. Company lawyers should not be too conservative in the use of these modern inventions and their many possibilities, always keeping in mind the words of the famous German philosopher Leibnitz, who wrote as early as in 1671 ... 'it is unworthy of excellent men to lose hours like slaves in the labour of calculation, which could safely be relegated to anyone else if machines were used'.

Legal research by computer is of eminent importance for countries whose legal system is based largely on case law. But also in continental Europe the flood of legal publications made computerized law libraries necessary. In the Federal Republic of Germany the government initiated a system for the collection of legal information (titled JURIS). The intention is to store laws and regulations, court decisions and eventually legal literature in a computer which can be used not only by courts and government agencies, but also by

19. Norma S. Lee: 'Legal Administrators Plan Annual Meeting in Atlanta', New York Law Journal March 27, 1978, pp. 23, 31.
20. The importance of this subject is underlined by the fact that 'The Practical Use of Computer Technology in the Law Office' was an important topic at the Seventeenth Conference of the International Bar Association in Sidney, Australia, 1978.

law offices and company legal departments.[21]

Access to legal information is facilitated and time and costs are saved. The popular image of the lawyer laboriously searching in mountains of dusty books may soon be a phantom of the past.

The work of the legal profession is closely connected with the interpretation and communication of words, whether typed, handwritten, printed or spoken. Any material change or development in the means of word communication, and text handling are of utmost importance to lawyers. Therefore, the invention of the typewriter, followed by the electric typewriter and the modern dictating machines greatly increased the communicative capacity of the lawyer. The most modern automatic memory typewriters, called 'Word Processors', permit the magnetic storage of frequently used texts and enable a typist with suitable training to correct and amend these texts.[22] The text can be retrieved from the memory equipment at any time and it is reproduced by printing equipment. Thus, any number of drafts can be made without retyping the entire document. Most word processing systems can also store volumes of frequently used segments of texts. This permits the attorney to create documents by combining stored texts with variable text where required.

The time required to type a letter or document is not changed by word processing; but if revisions are necessary, an automatic typewriter can cut the time of a second draft by 50% or more. For longer documents even more time is saved. With a stored 'library' of commonly used paragraphs and phrases, a word processing operator can construct documents or contracts by calling on the text in the proper order and printing out the document on a high-speed printer. To save time and make sure that documents are free of errors, word processing machines can sometimes automatically mark the lines or pages that have been revised so that the attorney has to read only those portions of the document which were changed from the previous draft.

Recent studies have concluded that one typist operating with a word processing machine can produce as many lines of text as three typists with conventio-

---

21. JURIS, Juristisches Informationssystem, Beilage 18/1978 des Bundesanzeigers, August 1, 1978.

22. Some articles on this subject:

Bernard Sternin, 'A Program for Typing Case Data Automatically', The Practical Lawyer, Volume 23 – No. 1, 1977.

Bernard Sternin, 'A System's Method for Recording Documents', The Practical Lawyer, Volume 23 – No. 4, 1977.

Marjorie A. Miller, 'How 16 Typists do Word Processing for a Law Firm with 126 Attorneys', New York Law Journal, March 22, 1977, page 21.

Willoughby Ann Walshe, 'New Equipment Digest: Speeding the Paper Flow', New York Law Journal, May 24, 1977, page 4.

'Law Office Automation', TELETEXT Communication Corp., 1977.

Robert S. Arthur, 'The Computer and the Practice of Law: Litigation Support', American Bar Association Journal, December 1977, page 1737.

'Word Processing and Law Firms', Pennsylvania Law Journal, April 24, 1978, page 10.

nal typewriters. Individual secretaries may divide their time between typing and performing functions such as telephoning and filing. This survey has also shown that in one law firm over 6,000 pages of text were produced per week by this system.

In the last twelve years hundreds of legal departments and law firms have purchased at least some sort of word processing equipment, but as with any major investment it is necessary to plan the organizational structure thoroughly and carefully, and to find out the right equipment for the use intended. The equipment is available, which makes the choice complicated, but assures, on the other hand, that a system can be found that will closely match the needs of the use envisioned.

The actual method of employing word processing equipment will necessarily vary from firm to firm. Most economical seems to be centralizing the equipment for efficient secretarial use. Centralization makes it easier to ensure that the equipment is kept busy. Regular and intensive training of the users is required to ensure the highest possible standard of productivity.

There is no doubt that law office technology will be developed further. The changing economic factors which demand automation in legal work will bring many transitional problems. But as all companies have to adapt to the new technological possibilities, so have the legal departments. The company lawyer, who is working in his company side by side with computer and automation specialist, has to be the spearhead of the legal profession in changing working methods and automating legal work as far as possible.

Good management of a legal department, optimal organization and the use of procedures and machines will successfully implement the talent of the legal and non-legal personnel.[23] This will result in efficiency and economy and it will further the standing of the department in its company.

D. Control Methods for Legal Departments

1. Checklist for Auditing a Company Law Department

In connection with acquisitions it is sometimes important to determine what has been done by the acquired company and which methods should be used to integrate the acquired companies' procedures into the acquiring company. One task of the legal department involved is to make a Legal Audit of the corporate affairs of the acquired company. This is done through a question-

23. For literature on law office management:
The Practical Lawyer's Law Office Management Manual Nr. 3, 1972. This volume includes a selection of articles on law office management systems and methods of streamlining law office procedure.
Bradford W. Hildebrandt, 'Managing the Small or Medium Law Office', Practicing Law Institute, New York City 1976.
Bradford W. Hildebrandt, 'Law Office Economics and Management', Practicing Law Institute, New York City 1977.

naire which can be adapted and used as a checklist for the legal department in order to study its accomplishments and shortcomings.[24]

A part of this questionnaire deals with affairs of the legal department. After looking into a breakdown of the budget of the legal departments, the organizational chart showing positions and chain of authority is important. Furthermore, in this respect the question has to be answered whether members of the legal department are admitted to the Bar of the state in which they normally live. In addition, company policy regarding application to local bar associations is one of the questions involved. No doubt in this connection it is important to ask which members of the company law department have a private law practice and how many hours they normally spend each month in this practice. Continuing legal education is important to maintain a high professional standard for the members of the legal department. Therefore, the checklist not only asks for details of legal education undertaken during the past year, but also lists publications and/or lectures which members of the legal department have given during the past five years. This permits the persons evaluating the checklist to see whether members of the legal department are capable of doing scientific work and legal research.

In this respect it is not surprising that there is also a question of how many volumes the law library has and under which categories these volumes come. The importance of law libraries becomes obvious if one reads that the law department of Prudential Insurance Company of America has in its Newark Headquarters the largest law library in New Jersey, after Rutgers Law School, with over 40,000 volumes. Nationwide, company law libraries in the United States aggregate about 100,000 volumes.[25]

The questions concerning the legal department permit − if the answers are properly and fully given − an evaluation, not only of the formal situation of the legal department, but also of the capability of the General Counsel and the attorneys.

2. Internal Control Procedures

Different in purpose but similar in result are internal control procedures for company law departments and law firms. As departments grow in size it is necessary to have more formality and to lay down standards and procedures in writing. The day-to-day activity of attorneys in a legal department resembles more a form of parallel play than a well-coordinated group activity. Working closely together should create in due course of time a department 'style'. This can be achieved through frequent personal contact and example. Contact with young attorneys and advice given by more experienced colleagues will

24. Burton H. Patterson, 'A Legal Audit Questionnaire', The Business Lawyer January 1971, pp. 983-996.
25. Quintin Johnstone and Dan Hopson, op. cit., p. 224.

create an esprit de corps which enables the young attorney to become part of a team and to act towards his 'clients' in the company as *the* representative of the company legal department. The observance of certain rules and principles by all members of the department strengthens the position of the department within the company.

A legal department has no quotas, no production stands, no efficiency index or even a common ground for comparison with other legal departments. The closest thing to a standard that exists is the yearly budget, but comparison of budgets will not say anything about the effectiveness of a legal department. One possible approach to measure effectiveness is the application of Results Oriented Planning to Legal Departments.[26]

The activities of the average legal department are controlled by outsiders because the department reacts to situations which are brought to it by outsiders. Only in very few cases does it act itself for instance preventive measures taken by the department). On the other hand the legal department is a staff and not a line function; and therefore, a number of problems are identical to those faced by managers in operating divisions. Hence, the legal department should always ask itself whether problems can be solved in a much easier way and it should not only look at problems, but also see opportunities. For instance, standard contracts can be drafted so that these standard forms can be utilized to facilitate work. The company lawyer must function not only as a lawyer − worker, but also as a lawyer − manager. Proper managing can save work and time. He can delegate and work through others. As a manager who can utilize Results Oriented Planning he has to set goals, standards, plans and controls to run his department. One goal, for instance, can be to reduce the number of signatures required or to reduce insurance premiums paid by the company for certain types of insurance. Since few business departments are as autonomous as a legal department, it is very difficult to measure the effectiveness of the department. On the other hand the only criterion for a legal department is its effectiveness. The purpose of results oriented planning is to increase such effectiveness.

The effectiveness can also be increased by internal regulations for the department: for example, the rule that the department head or his deputy must always be in the building, or that the department must always have a number of lawyers in the building in case of urgent business, antitrust action or similar events.

Another rule could be that any operating man may interrupt a lawyer at any time to discuss urgent matters with him. The problem of the client is more important than the work of the lawyer.

A very important rule can be a deadline on all advertising and product-copy review. Advertising copy review is especially important in consumer goods companies and demands a certain amount of time. Unfortunately advertising

---

26. Alan D. Choka, 'The Effective Legal Department: A Primer of Results Oriented Planning', The Business Lawyer April 1969, pp. 825-875.

agencies present the copy to be reviewed at very short notice to the legal department. Therefore, rules can be established to make sure that legal personnel is at all times available to review these copies; furthermore, the rules should state that not only the legal department, but also the technical departments review advertising copy to enable the company lawyer to certify that product properties which are claimed in advertising are correct. This is even more important under the forthcoming legislation in many European countries which holds companies liable for the truth of advertising statements. Another rule will be that all letters or memorandums must be acknowledged or handled within 24 hours or some other fixed period of time. This avoids delay in handling this material.[27]

3. Company Law Department Manual

Company Law Departments have to abide by the internal rules and regulations existing in the company to which they belong. These rules and regulations will regulate working conditions, office hours, handling of expense reports and invoices, travel arrangement, vacation policy, salary, employee benefit plan arrangements, housekeeping, etc. In other words, regulations normally applicable for the entire company personnel also apply to the personnel of the company law department.

For the specific work done in this organizational unit, it is helpful to have a company law department manual. This manual contains suggestions and instructions for work procedures. It is obvious that companies' practices and procedures vary. Therefore, it is necessary to tailor such a manual to each company law department's needs.

The law department manual will be used primarily by new company attorneys, but its development should not be restricted to such a use. It should be a mirror of the existing policies of the law department and it will, in essence, force the law department to make decisions that are aimed at establishing instructions and practices for all its employees. This will make the operation of the entire department more productive and efficent. Many benefits result from the process of preparing such a manual because this is the opportunity to review the actual work of the department. In addition, the manual will be a valuable and functional reference source for all members of the law department. The Corporation Law Committee of the Young Lawyers' Section of the American Bar Association in cooperation with the Corporate Law Departments' Committee, Corporation, Banking and Business Law Section, developed in 1971 a model for a corporate law department. This manual has been adapted by the author to European needs and conditions and it is attached hereto. It is a guideline and model of a manual taking into considera-

27. Alan D. Choka, 'The Role of Corporate Counsel', The Business Lawyer April 1970, pp. 1011-1026.

tion the special needs of a law department and supplementing the personnel rules and regulations existing in the company as far as the special necessities of the law department are concerned.

It might be added that large American law firms also operate with such manuals. These manuals also include the personnel rules applicable to the entire personnel of the firms.

I would like to mention one point which can either be included in a manual or a separate policy statement/advice to employees:

Legal Departments are not set up for the purpose of giving advice to employees of the company in connection with their personal problems. The General Counsel is not the General Welfare Legal Adviser of the staff of the company. Normally the company lawyer is so occupied with the affairs of his employer that he does not have sufficient time to handle adequatly the personal problems of other employees of the company.

But the problem has also an ethical aspect. Company lawyers who are members of their national bar have to be very careful in giving free advice to company employees because in most countries rules concerning professional ethics prohibit such advice. Such rules exist in the Federal Republic of Germany and the United States of America, the two countries where most members of company legal departments are admitted to the bar. There are also laws prohibiting unauthorized practice of the law. To avoid problems and embarrassment for the individual company lawyer, it is advisable to establish a clear policy for the legal department that prohibits the giving of free legal advice to company employees.[28]

28. Richard S. Maurer, 'Ethical and Legal Problems of the Corporate Counsel in the Rendering of Personal Advice to Company Officers and Employees', The Business Lawyer April 1966, pp. 817-828.

Annex:
Model Company Law Department Manual

Section I. ORGANIZATION OF LAW DEPARTMENT

1.10 Organization Chart

Section II. SCOPE OF LAW DEPARTMENT ACTIVITIES

2.10 Objectives of Law Department
2.20 Special Functions of Law Department
    2.21 Advice and Counsel
    2.22 The Company's Operations
    2.23 Laws and Regulations Affecting Company's Operations
    2.24 Pending or Proposed Legislation
    2.25 Formulating Policies and Procedures to Guide Operating Departments in Avoiding Legal Difficulties
    2.26 Keeping Informed of Practices of Other Companies
2.30 Law Department Assignments – Practice and Procedure
    2.31 General Responsibilities of Each Attorney
        a. Become Familiar With Company's Operations and Laws and Regulations Applicable to Those Operations
        b. Keep Current as to Recent Decisions and Other Source Materials
        c. Assist Operating Departments
        d. Initiate Action
        e. Consult With General Counsel
        f. Keep General Counsel, Management and Other Officials Informed
        g. Become Familiar With Standard Contracts, Practices and Procedures
        h. Establishing Legal Files
        i. Delegation of Authority Upon Attorney's Absence
        j. Maintain Confidentiality and Privilege
    2.32 Specific Subject Matters and Procedures for Handling
        a. Antitrust
        b. Claims
        c. Contracts
        d. Company Law and Financial Statements
        e. Labor and Employee Relations
        f. Litigation
        g. Security and Criminal Matters
        h. Patents, Copyrights and Trademarks
        i. Real Estate
        j. Tax
2.40 Relations with Other Departments
    2.41 Routine Matters
    2.42 Internal Communications

Section I. ORGANIZATION OF THE LAW DEPARTMENT

1.10 Organization Chart
(Organization Chart of the Law Department would be placed in this section).

Section II. SCOPE OF LAW DEPARTMENT ACTIVITIES

2.10 Objectives of the Law Department

2.20 Special Functions of Law Department

2.21 Advice and Counsel
The Law Department is charged with the responsibility of advising the company with respect to all legal matters.

2.22 The Company's Operations
The Law Department has a continuing responsibility to monitor and review the legal aspects of the company's operations so as to be able to advise the management and employees of the company.

2.23 Laws and Regulations Affecting the Company's Operations
The Law Department should be aware of applicable federal, state and local laws and regulations which could affect the company's operations.

2.24 Pending or Proposed Legislation
The Law Department may have responsibility, along with other departments, (a) for monitoring pending and proposed legislation, (b) for advising appropriate departments of the significance thereof, and (c) for recommending changes in such legislation.

2.25 Formulating Policies and Procedures to Guide Operating Departments in Avoiding Legal Difficulties
The Law Department can serve an important function in a preventative role by initiating policies and procedures for consideration by other departments that will help to avoid legal difficulties.

2.26 Keeping Informed as to the Practices of Other Companies
The Law Department, through such means as bar association activities and continuing legal education seminars, should keep well advised of current procedures and methods used by other companies in dealing with legal problems.

2.30 Law Department Assignments – Practice and Procedure

2.31 General Responsibilities of Each Attorney
a. Become familiar with company's operations and laws and regulations applicable to those operations. Operations include the company's corporate structure, contracts, licenses, etc. Attorneys should be familiar with the specific laws, ordinances, regulations, etc., in their assigned areas of responsibility.
b. Keep current as to recent decisions and other source materials. Journals, law reviews and other periodicals subscribed to by the company or firm law library should be circulated among requesting attorneys in the office. Items not subscribed to by the library can often be obtained by the librarian from other sources upon request of an attorney. Each attorney may wish to receive all such materials covering his area of practice. From time to time memoranda or reviews of specific cases, articles, notes, etc. should be circulated generally. In addition, office meetings are held from time to time at which legal matters of current interest or concern are discussed.

c. Assist operating departments. Advice and assistance should be provided to operating departments in each attorney's area of responsibility. In addition to responding to specific requests for assistance of information, attorneys must have sufficient knowledge of the operations of the company to be able to recognize potential legal problems.

d. Initiate action. The Law Department shall initiate legal action upon request or concurrence of management.

e. Consult with General Counsel. In any case involving new policy, consultation should be held with the General Counsel. The General Counsel should also be consulted in matters concerning which he wishes to be kept advised and with respect to such other matters as in the attorney's opinion, are of sufficient importance to warrant the General Counsel's attention.

f. Keep General Counsel, management and other officials informed. Activities of the Law Department should be documented. A written memorandum of all contacts with outside counsel and of interdepartmental conferences should be made and placed in the file. A written report on every file for which an attorney is responsible should be sent to the General Counsel and any other official in the company interested in the matter in question at the time any major decision or action is taken.

g. Become familiar with standard contracts, practices and procedures. Important company contracts and documents, together with various form files and other written procedures are often located at numerous places within the company. Inasmuch as these items often provide essential reference or starting point material, a list of such items and their locations should be contained in an appendix and reference made to that appendix under this subtopic.

h. Establish legal files. Legal files are established for each case or other legal matter involving the company. Each attorney should become familiar with the filing and indexing system.

i. Delegation of authority upon attorney's absence. In the event of planned absences, an attorney should consult with the General Counsel so that responsibility for and authority over work can continue.

j. Maintain confidentiality and privilege. All information conveyed to the attorney by the client, other than that which is of general knowledge in the community or is cleared for further publication of some sort by the client, must be held in confidence. Any doubts must be resolved in favor of the confidential nature of the information.

Comment: Attorneys are often more familiar with the internal affairs of the company than anyone other than management and directors. Because they are privy to information not known to the general public, they are a prime target of those seeking confidential or privileged information for any of the numerous reasons such information is sought. The individual attorney must be ever diligent not to fall prey so such individuals.

2.32 Specific Subject Matters and Procedures for Handling

An informational sheet should be prepared showing the names, office and telephone numbers of each attorney, and designating the major areas of law handled by that attorney. A short description of the matters encompassed under the general headings should also be included. The sheet should also designate an alternative name, in the event that the attorney primarily responsible is not available. If the sheet is to be used as a reference by other departments, consideration should be given to describing in some detail the functions performed by the designated attorneys. This sheet will also be used by each attorney when it is necessary to bring in other Law Department attorneys for advice and assistance in handling a matter involving several areas of law.

a. Antitrust. Antitrust implications or involvement may be indicated in the following type of company activity: lease agreements, franchise agreements, acquisitions, mergers, etc.

b. Claims. Claims concerning (example of action, or service or product involved) should be referred to the following: (individuals, departments). No litigation should be commenced without the concurrence/recommendation of the following: (individuals, committee(s), etc.). An analysis of claims involving (matter) should be made by the designated attorney and sent to the following: (individuals, committee(s), etc.).

Customer Matters and Consumer Complaints. Policies will vary according to the companies' products, services and line of business. For each major product or service line, specific instructions should be included for handling customer requests or complaints. Types of

114

complaints frequently received could be categorized and the names and telephone numbers of supervisors responsible for handling included. Procedures for handling matters where litigation is indicated or appears imminent should be treated with particular care.

Claim Processing. Procedures here should be established and understood by all departmental personnel having customer contacts. Consider training sessions or slide show presentations.

Referral of Complaints to Other Departments. Claims should be identified, categorized, and referred promptly. Prompt handling by the responsible department is essential. Liaison between this department and the designated attorney should be followed.

Liaison with Insurers. Familiarity by attorney with insurance contracts in force; coverage; and provisions therein, detailing notification, is essential. Notification procedures should be established within the company and between it and its insurer(s).

Insurance Coverage. If a particular loss or injury is covered under an existing insurance policy, whether it be a liability, property damage, workmen's compensation, products liability or any other type policy, the entire case should immediately be reported to the insurer or insurance broker who would handle the matter from beginning to end. In such instances the attorney should not attempt to obtain a release or make any payments or promises of payments, even if the insurance coverage is questionable, as such action would invalidate the insurance.

Insurance and Claims by Companies Against Third Parties. As a general rule, an attorney should never obtain or attempt to obtain a release or sign any release on behalf of the company, except in the case of a strictly commercial loss or minor property damage claim where there is no possible exposure to a personal injury claim. Special attention should be given to procedures for referring personal injury cases, major property damage situations and claims for false arrest or false imprisonment to the appropriate attorney or to outside counsel.

c. Contracts. (A more extensive development of this topic has been done for illustrative purposes.)

Preparation of Contracts. Responsibilities for preparation and procedures for discussing and reviewing drafts can be described.

Authorizations and Use of Outside Counsel. Assistance from outside counsel in the preparation of contracts should be obtained in accordance with the procedures described in Section III. If outside parties will be involved in the contract, and any negotiation of contract terms is to take place, the role of outside counsel in such negotiations should be firmly established. All factual information available and pertinent to the transaction should be transmitted to outside counsel.

Routing to Proper Executives and Employees. Contract drafts which are circulated must carefully be reviewed for oversights, problem clauses, and necessary inclusions. Sufficient copies should be sent to appropriate executives, members of the company legal staff and outside counsel. Consideration should be given to preparing a checklist of important items for analysis by each person on the route list. A deadline for return of contract copies with comments should be indicated on the checklist or transmittal note. The appropriate executives who would review certain types of contracts or other documents should be specified. Note: Consider obtaining review of important contracts by specialists in tax and antitrust regulations.

Securing Necessary Approvals. When all contract copies have been returned with comments, the attorney should carefully sift through these comments and review the contract in light of such comments, rewriting where and when necessary. A final draft of the contract should then be prepared, and submitted to those persons whose approvals are necessary.

Execution. Once all necessary approvals of the final contract draft have been obtained, the attorney should prepare a checklist of details needed to execute the agreement; e.g., powers of attorney, affidavits, company authorizations of signatory parties, numbers of contract copies needed, etc. If any changes have been written or otherwise entered upon the final contract, approval for these changes should be obtained from the appropriate executives and other parties involved. Once executed, the contract should be checked for minor omissions, accuracy of dates, and state and local governmental references. Copies should then be provided to the appropriate persons.

Closing Instructions. Checklists are helpful for this purpose and should be filled out as to amounts, descriptions, terms, etc. Where tasks have been performed by several individuals or attorneys, their names should be indicated with the functions they performed.

Directive for the Signing (Execution) of Agreements. The Company Law Department has to make sure that all agreements and commitments to which the company is a party are properly signed. The authority granted for the signature of such documents will be governed by the legal system of the country involved.

Comment: In Common Law countries such as the United Kingdom and the United States of America, the officers of the company normally sign legally binding documents and in these countries it is usual to have one signature representing the company. Some European countries require either by law or company statute two signatures. In these countries the law defines the extent of the authority of certain categories of company officials.

It is advisable for the Company Law Department to draft and publish within the company a directive or rule defining the authority and conditions for such signatures. This directive or rule should include the statement that the Company Law Department is responsible for all formalities required in the country. In particular it has to make sure that all decisions and authorizations of the Board of Directors or the corresponding company organ have been obtained and documented before the signature(s) are affixed to the document.

In the directive or rule it is advisable to include the suggestion that members of the Company Law Department participate in the negotiations and drafting of contracts as early as possible. Thus the Company Law Department can certify the correctness of the agreement as to form and legal requirements.

In countries requiring only one signature the certificate of the Legal Department is shown by affixing a stamp or the initial of one of the attorneys. In countries with double signature, one of the signatures is given by a member of the Law Department, and in all important cases by the General Counsel.

Filing and Recording. Procedures for filing or recording of signed contracts and documents are most important to avoid loss or confusion. All such documents should be safeguarded in the Company Law Department where a director of records and his assistants are responsible. All important documents should be kept in fireproof filing cabinets with copies to be guarded in a different location.

If centralized record filing is not possible (for instance subsidiary companies in different countries must retain documents for local inspection by authorities) copies should be kept in the Law Department. Thus it is possible for the Law Department to control the observation of all formalities required under local law and to record all important legal business of the subsidiary.

Access to confidential documents has to be regulated. Directives on this subject should include rules regarding duplication of such files.

The increasing volume of files requires regulations on the life time of company records. The time for which company records must be preserved is prescribed in many countries by tax laws or bookkeeping regulations. The Legal Department should notify in regular intervals all management units of the company on the storage times contained in these laws for the various categories of company records.

Historically important records and documents should not be destroyed but handed over to the company historian for his archives.

Maintenance und Files. Established procedure should be outlined here, with guides which could be followed by secretaries and file clerks, e.g., transmittals, original and number of copies, withdrawals, indexing, etc.

d. Company Law and Financial Statements. Disclosures and News Releases. In addition to other information or instructions under this heading describing procedures for handling news releases, this section should contain an up-to-date outline of existing rules regarding disclosure. Recent case law concerning the liabilities of executives and directors and company insiders should also be summarized here. Consideration should be given to preparing a memorandum to other departments and divisions concerning the desirability of clearing disclosures and news releases with the Law Department.

Company Documents. The Law Department may have responsibility for the preparation and filing of the following documents: (When appropriate, procedures describing the handling of these matters should be indicated.)

1. Notices and minutes of Stockholder, Director, Executive and Financial Committee meetings.
2. Proxy statements and proxies which are regulated.
3. Annual or other filings in the state of incorporation and in which the corporation is registered to do business.
4. Securities Act and Securities Exchange Act filings, review of Registration Statements and amendments thereto.
5. Communications by company during or immediately preceding registrations.
6. Inside information procedures.
7. Pension, profit-sharing, and other deferred compensation plans, procedures and records.

Financial Statements. The Law Department should review the following documents pursuant to an annual checklist:

1. Annual and quarterly reports.
2. Annual and other periodic financial statements.
3. Dividend communications.
4. Acquisitions and mergers including tax, company law, antitrust, securities, accounting and others (considerations) onit.
5. Public offerings.
6. Private placements.
7. Legal aspects of investments.

e. Labor and Employee Relations. The Law Department may be responsible for (1) assisting management in negotiating and preparing contracts with unions, (2) determining compliance by union with contract provisions, and (3) becoming familiar with federal and state labour laws affecting the company's labour and employee relations, including wage and hour laws and federal and state safety laws.

f. Litigation. A more extensive development of this topic has been done for illustrative purposes. Law Departments generally have well-developed procedures and practices for handling claims, suits, and other matters involving litigation against and for the company. The following list is a sample.

Service of Lawsuits. It is imperative that the details of the service of lawsuits be determined as soon as possible so that the company will not be in default for failing to answer within the allotted time. If service of lawsuit is effected upon a local office of the company, the date, time of service, upon whom, names of plaintiff and defendant, state and court involved, time period in which to answer and name, address and telephone number of attorney for plaintiff, if indicated, should be immediately telephoned into the Law Department by the party responsible for the operation of the local office. All papers should also immediately be forwarded to the Law Department. If service is effected on outside counsel, obviously the details of the service are immediately known.

Preparation of Case. An attorney is charged with the responsibility for the proper handling of the case. If outside counsel has been retained, the attorney will help in the preparation of the case. Although the actual conduct of the trial should be left to outside counsel, the company attorney should work closely with him throughout the trial. Outside counsel should be responsible for the handling of the proceedings in the case, but the ultimate decisions as to whether to settle the case, take an appeal or to employ other policy decisions are the responsibility of the company's attorney or its General Counsel. The attorney can be of great assistance in bringing about contacts between outside counsel and the employees of the company involved in a case.

Review of Documents. The Law Department will review all pleadings and briefs prepared by outside counsel, and render assistance in petrial and trial proceedings.

Assistance in Trial of Case. The company attorney should be certain that outside counsel is adequately prepared and fully understands the company's position and particularly how the outcome of the case might affect the company's operations.

g. Security and Criminal Matters. All instances involving a possible crime by a company employee will be investigated initially by the Law Department. If the preliminary investigation indicates that a crime has been comitted, prosecution will be authorized only after consultation with and approval of General Counsel. The matter will then be turned over to local law enforcement officers for further investigation. As a general rule, in order to reduce the chances of a malicious prosecution suit, the corporation will not act as the prosecuting party, although the Law Department will cooperate fully with law enforcement officers in conducting their investigation and in supplying witnesses for any criminal trial proceeding.

h. Patents, Copyrights and Trademarks. A more extensive development of this topic has been done for illustrative purposes.

Copyright. Clients involved in design or in publishing or other communications industries have diverse copyright problems which go far beyond the scope of a company checklist, but every company lawyer should be aware of the following areas in which copyright protection may be helpful:

1. Catalogs and Brochures. Any pamphlet which is worth your client's printing cost is probably worth copyrighting. Illustrations in a catalog may include designs or plans which should be protected from direct copying. Intrafirm publications may include material which would prove embarrassing if published out of context in the press. Copyright does not insure power of control. The statute requires "prompt" deposit with the Copyright Office of two copies of a copyrighted work and makes deposit and registration a condition precedent to the bringing of suit for infringement. However, as the courts have permitted complaintants to comply with the deposit and registration requirements immediately prior to bringing suit, it is probably safe with respect to minor publications to delay deposit and registratrion until an actual controversy arises.

2. Advertisements. While mere labled and brand names are not copyrightable, original graphic and textual material contained in advertisements generally are. Copyright may be useful to protect advertisements against parody or other misuse or against close copying by competitors. The copyright notice printed in the front of a magazine or newspaper generally does not protect advertisements.

Trademarks and Trade Names

1. Trade and Service Marks. Brand names, and house marks used to promote and identify products or services are generally registrable as trademarks or service marks. Registration in principal foreign countries may be required by clients in the world market. The procuring of a trademark registration involves significant expense, and judgment must be applied to determine whether statutory protection is warranted for a particular brand name or logo. It should be kept in mind that in some foreign countries all rights may be lost in the absence of a timely registration.

2. Trade Names. A company's name may sometimes be registrable as a trade or service mark. Often, abbreviations of the name are registered. The Law Department makes sure that only abbreviations are used which correspond with the registered trademarks.

i. Real Estate. Generally, files containing forms of contracts, agreements, clauses, etc., should be established and indexed. Reference should be made to the nature, scope and source of these files. Instructions as to procedures for keeping the files updated and for indexing new matters should be set out under this heading.

j. Tax. Procedures for handling tax matters generally have been established and should be described under this topic. Some companies may have a tax department with its own established procedures. Adequate instructional information should include references to personnel, source of documents, etc.

2.40 Relations With Other Departments

The Law Department does not issue mandates, directives or instructions to the other departments of the company. Its function is to assist, advise and suggest, not to direct. Generally, it is not the function of the Law Department to determine or decide questions of business policy, although its members may play a material role in helping company management to formulate such policy. Many proposed courses of action may involve some legal risk. Where this is so, the attorney must attempt to devise ways of eliminating or minimizing the legal risk. If the risk cannot be entirely eliminated, the attorney should give a frank evaluation of the risk. Responsibility for evaluation of the risk cannot be passed on the others on the grounds that it is a 'business decision'. Other departments cannot be expected to judge how real a legal risk may be. They want the assistance of the Law Department in determining whether the risk should be taken.

2.41 Routine Matters
Routine for routing, advice to other departments, issuance of legal opinions, and referrals should be given under this heading.

2.42 Internal Communications
The attorney-client relationship should be preserved on internal communications. In some instances, this may require special captions to some documents, e.g., 'prepared for use of counsel in connection with Smith v. Co.'.

2.43 Topical Seminars and Meetings
Consideration should be given to holding seminars or special informational/educational meetings for departments or clients. These have value to lawyers and clients alike and may serve to prevent future legal problems.

2.50 Legal Assistance to Employees

Generally, a company cannot and does not undertake to furnish legal services to its employees. It is contrary to company policy for its attorneys to represent employees in personal matters. Nevertheless, there inevitably will be occasions when individual employees will want to discuss personal problems with certain attorneys. The Law Department obviously should be as courteous and helpful as possible. When approached with such personal problems, attorneys may give whatever suggestions or assistance may be possible short of legal advice or representation. A discussion of the Law Department's policies may include the following:

Section III. OUTSIDE COUNSEL

3.10 Areas of Consultation

The objectives of retaining outside counsel are (1) to strengthen the overall capabilities of the Law Department by enabling company attorneys to concentrate on legal matters involving peculiar knowledge and skill as to the company's operations, and (2) to ensure the competent handling of certain legal matters requiring special knowledge or skill.
The General Counsel should be consulted prior to contacting outside counsel. Established procedures will generally designate (1) outside counsels which have been approved for handwork of a particular nature, (2) details for referring bills for review before payment, and (3) the manner of handling copies of opinions or other work products of outside counsel. The following is a list of areas in which Law Departments have traditionally retained outside counsel. This list is not exhaustive and is merely a suggested format for drafting this Section of the manual.
a. Antitrust
b. Legislation and Public Affairs
c. Litigation. Court work involves special acquaintance with local judges and jurors. Most court work will be referred to outside counsel. Guides as to the type of court work to be handled by the Law Department should be described. Whether to retain outside counsel for appearances before administrative agencies should be decided on a case-by-case basis giving considerat-

ion to the nature of the problem; the availability of outside counsel; the indicated preference, if any, of the agency; and the experience of house counsel. In selecting outside trial counsel, the company should consider, among other things, the general reputation of said counsel, their reputation in the specific field of law involved and previous experience with said counsel. Fees to be charged by the outside counsel should be discussed at the outset of the retention to avoid any disagreement later. For matters which will continue over a period of time, it might be well to have outside counsel bill on a quarterly basis.

d. Patents, Trademarks, Copyrights

e. Questions of Applicable Law. When a company operates on an international, multistate or multilocational basis, legal problems involving remote locations, countries or states will from time to time arise. Questions of law may arise which should be referred to outside counsel in the appropriate location. Any such referral should be closely analyzed by the company attorney to insure that the problem is significant enough to warrant referral. It may be desirable to retain outside counsel for (1) analysis of local law including such questions as whether or not it is advisable to qualify in a particular state where the company has some business transactions; (2) analyses of the impact of the applicable laws, conflicts of laws, and jurisdictional questions; (3) interpretations of local law; (4) analysis of problems which are broad and complex, or problems which involve specialized areas of legal knowledge; and (5) their knowledge or skill in handling matters before certain agencies, courts or other governmental bodies.

f. Tax Matters. Tax law is complex and constantly changes. Unless the company employs a tax specialist, capable outside assistance may be necessary for the proper handling of any significant tax matters.

g. Other Matters. Occasionally, a situation will arise in which the attorney senses that legal consequences are involved, but because of unfamiliarity with the situation or the area of law in which the legal consequences will manifest themselves, cannot fairly render reasoned advice. Legal reserch is an excellent tool, but the attorney should never rely on such research for the entire legal framework of a particular problem. Since research is only a tool for use within a framework already established by an attorney's education and experience, a problem which falls outside that framework should immediately be considered for reference to outside counsel. Unusual matters, which fall outside the framework of any company attorney, might include onetime matters such as mergers, 'going public', trademark and patent problems, or an unusual theory of potential liability which the attorney has developed and desires to 'check out' with outside counsel.

3.20 Procedure and Record of Matters Referred to Outside Counsel

Before any retainer or employment agreement is made with outside counsel, the following matters should be discussed information thereto carefully considered.

3.21 Conflicts of Interest

The professional judgment of the company attorney should be exercised, within the bounds of the law, solely for the benefit of his employer-client and free of compromising influences of loyalties. Accordingly, in selecting outside counsel to represent the company, and in working with outside counsel, the company attorney should be certain that the most effective outside legal assistance is utilized. Of course, the wishes of company executives and financial cost to the company should always be given appropriate consideration by the company attorney in selecting or working with outside counsel.

Although the company attorney offers his services to only his employer, the ethical considerations between the company attorney and the company are synonymous with the ethical considerations of outside counsel who normally have multiple employers. Accordingly, in selecting or dealing with outside counsel, the company attorney must represent his employer with undivided fidelity. Except with the consent of his employer-client, after full disclosure, he should not exercise his professional judgment on behalf of the company, if he will be, or reasonably may be, influenced by his own financial, business, property, or personal interests.

120

Thus, except with the consent of the company after full disclosure, the company attorney should not refer legal work to, or work with, an outside law firm if: he hopes to later join that firm; he has previously been a member of the firm; close friends or relatives are members of the firm; the outside firm may provide free assistance to the company attorney in a personal matter; the claim is against an entity in which the company attorney has an interest, and he wishes a poor job be done; or for any other similar 'financial, business, property, or personal interests'.

In summary, the professional judgment of the company attorney should be independently exercised and used solely for the benefit of the company.

3.22 Procedures for Referral

When the attorney deems it necessary that the company retain outside counsel, he should discuss the situation with the General Counsel. If outside counsel has been retained in that jurisdiction previously, he should call this to the attention of the General Counsel to determine whether or not it is desired that the same outside counsel be retained. If no outside counsel has previously been used in that jurisdiction, he should suggest to the General Counsel some law firms in that area which he believes are capable of representing the company. On receiving the General Counsel's approval of outside counsel, the attorney should contact the firm by telephone to determine whether or not the firm would be willing and able to represent the company. If telephone assurance is received, the attorney should then furnish a complete file to the outside counsel together with a brief resume of the applicable facts, any suggestions he might have as to the applicable law, and any specific action he might desire of the outside counsel. In addition he should request a confirming letter acknowledging receipt of the file and detailing the fee arrangement with such counsel. Outside counsel should also be instructed in all cases to send to the referring company all material in his file on the day of receipt.

3.23 Fees and Disbursements

On receiving from outside counsel a statement of fees and disbursements above a certain amount (to be agreed on internally in the Law Department) the attorney should advise the General Counsel whether or not he believes that the fee is justified. He should acquaint the General Counsel with the period of time the statement covers, what the outside counsel has done in that time, and the status of the case. For fees and disbursements below a certain amount, the attorney should be capable of determining whether or not the statement is proper.

3.24 Reporting, Control and Decisionmaking

While some matters will require periodic reporting more frequently than others, these report requirements should be established with outside counsel, e.g., 6 months on large claims, monthly on antitrust litigation, etc.

Outside counsel should not make any commitments for the company which could hamper future policy decisional-making ability unless specific permissions have been given. Authority for settlement terms should be expressly covered, preferably by written agreement with firms who have not handled legal business for the company before.

3.25 Internal Records and Handling

Company management and employees should be kept informed as to legal matters being handled by outside counsel to the same extent that they are informed concerning Law Department handled matters. See Section 2.31 (f).

3.26 Review and Appraisal of Outside Handling

The performance of outside counsel shall be reviewed periodically. If a member of the Law Department is not satisfied with the representation provided by outside counsel, he should discuss this matter with the General Counsel. Normally numerous considerations are present in reviewing and appraising the performance of outside counsel. For example, the general effectiveness of counsel, the amount of fees charged, the results in particular cases, and continuous contacts during the period of representation are all factors in reviewing and appraising outside counsel's performance. It will be a very rare case where the Law Department will deem it necessary to replace outside counsel during the handling of a case.

121

Section IV. CORRESPONDENCE

4.10 Incoming Correspondence

4.11 Delivery to Mail Department
Mail is delivered to the company (specify frequencies, times). All mail deliveries are made to the mail department which promptly sorts it (upon omit receipt). The messengers begin delivery of the mail (when). No mail is to be disturbed or interrupted before distribution except in extraordinary instances.

4.12 Mail Addressed to Particular Attorneys or Departments
All mail addressed to a particular attorney or department is to be delivered unopened to the attorney's 'in' box on his secretary's desk or to the department's 'in' box on the head secretary's desk. The secretary is to open the mail and clip all checks or loose enclosures to the letter and the envelope to avoid losing or misplacing them.

4.13 Publications, etc.
All publications, including magazines, and miscellaneous literature not specifically addressed to any individual will be opened at the mail department and delivered to the library. The library will shelve and file the material or attach route slips to it and circulate it as indicated by the card index covering circulation of publications which is maintained in the library.

4.14 Other Mail
Other mail, such as correspondence and statements, which is simply addressed to the Law Department and not to any particular attorney or department will be delivered to the office manager for further disposition.

4.15 Hand-delivered Mail
Mail which is delivered by outside messengers must be taken to the mail department. For security reasons, outside messengers are not to be permitted to make deliveries to particular attorneys or departments. The mail department will sort such mail and have it delivered in accordance with (specify procedures).

4.16 Time Stamp
Upon opening of mail it must be time-stamped. Secretaries are to time-stamp mail addressed to particular attorneys or departments. The library will date-stamp and company-name-stamp publications, advance sheets, etc. The office manager will route the other mail to the appropriate attorney or department at which point it will be stamped.

4.17 Attorney's Absence
When an attorney is away, the secretary should immediately direct his mail to the person who is handling the matter in the attorney's absence. Before the attorney leaves, he should dictate a memorandum as to disposition of his mail.
General Counsel's Absence. When the General Counsel is absent, his mail should be read by his immediate subordinate and appropriate action taken.

4.18 Collect Deliveries
The mail department should notify the attorney of any deliveries requiring payment of more than $ 10 and obtain his approval of payment.

4.19 Envelopes
Envelopes for mail addressed to particular attorneys or departments are to be saved by the secretary of office manager who opens them and delivered to the attorney or addressee together with the correspondence and enclosures. Only the attorney or addressee is to dispose of envelopes, whose postmarks or addresses may be very important in later disputes or negotiations.

122

4.20 Outgoing Correspondence

4.21 Proper Letterhead and Designation of Writer
It is important that the proper letterhead be utilized and that the writer's capacity be indicated. If attorneys are assigned to specific divisions and desire to identify closely with the division, they should use letterhead of that division. The appropriate title should also be indicated, whether it be attorney, counsel, assistant counsel, etc.

Comment: The use of proper letterhead is not only a matter of identification of the writer or company policy, but it also involves in many countries rules of professional conduct, which regulate the use of the professional title 'attorney at law' in connection with company business and, therefore, letterheads.
The Committee on Professional and Judicional Ethics of the New York Bar Association submitted in its opinion no. 892 a committee report on the use of letterheads by corporate law departments (The record of the Association of the Bar of the City of New York, volume 32, no. 9, December 1977, page 680).
In this opinion the committee states that a lawyer may not properly be party to what may well involve deception. A lawyer who is house counsel for the corporation must always use a letterhead identifying his connection with his corporate employer. He certainly need not do so if he is representing clients other than a corporation or is not corresponding on the corporations business, but house counsel should not fail to identify his connection with his corporate employer in a letterhead or in the text of a letter, if, under these circumstances, the failure would be likely to mislead the recipient of the letter.
In Europe members of the company law department will normally use regular company letterheads which are often marked with the name of the department. It should be rule that private letterheads of members of the company law department are not to be used for company correspondence. The rules of the German Bar Association (Grundsätze des anwaltlichen Standesrechts dated August 1, 1977) state expressly in § 40, that a Rechtsanwalt who is a salaried employee of a company may not use, in the correspondence of his employer, the title Rechtsanwalt. The reason for this rule can be seen in the independant position of the attorney who is supposed to have clients for which he does not act in an employee – employer relationship. The ethical rules govering this question are of course, different in each country and largely dependent on the integration of company lawyers in the local Bar.

4.22 Copies to General Counsel and File
If established procedures require, General Counsel should receive copies of correspondence which involve matters which may significantly affect the company's business and of which he should be aware. There should be a file copy of all correspondence.

4.23 Outside Counsel
Outside counsel should receive a copy of all correspondence relative to the matters on which he is representing the company, so long as no confidential information is contained therein.

4.24 Communications Signed by General Counsel or Company Secretary
In some cases, it might be appropriate for the General Counsel or the Company Secretary to sign correspondence rather than a member of the Law Department. In this event, the lawyer involved should prepare the letter for signature by the General Counsel or Company Secretary.

4.25 Addresses
The address should indicate where the attorney who is writing is located, which may not necessarily be the division's headquarters.

4.26 Distribution of Copies Within Company
Copies should be distributed to those individuals who are involved and concerned with the particular matter.

4.27 Confirming Oral Opinions

If requested, oral opinions should be confirmed in writing; and, in this event, the question presented should also be in writing.

4.28 Requests for Information

In requesting information, the attorney should indicate the reason for the request.

4.29 Unassigned Areas of Operation

These areas should be assigned to an attorney with due consideration of work load and expertise that may be required.

4.30 Circulation Within the Department

4.31 General

The following procedures assume that copies of all correspondence will be received by the General Counsel. The attorney originating or receiving a particular piece of correspondence is to judge whether it concerns a routine matter or a matter of sufficient interest to other members of the Law Department. A conscientious effort should be made to cut down on the circulation of correspondence of no particular significance or interest to other attorneys.

4.32 Incoming Correspondence

The addressee attorney receiving the original, or the attorney receiving the only copy of such correspondence directed to a member of the Law Department, or (if two or more attorneys receive copies of a particular piece of correspondence and the original is directed to someone outside the department) the attorney whose name appears first in the list of persons receiving copies, shall make the dicision as to the disposition of such correspondence. The other attorney or attorneys receiving copies shall retain them for their own reference, if desired, or destroy them. The attorney making the decision as to the disposition of incoming correspondence shall indicate such disposition in the upper right-hand corner of the correspondence, as follows:
'File' marked on correspondence denotes that that particular piece of correspondence goes to:
'Circ.' marked on correspondence denotes that that particular piece of correspondence goes to:

4.33 Outgoing Correspondence

The attorney originating a particular piece of correspondence shall make the decision as to the disposition of the file copy, following the same procedure outlined for 'Incoming Correspondence'. The correspondence shall be returned to the originating attorney for filing.
The 'file' copy only will be marked for filing or circulation and in particular instances where it is desired to supply a copy to another member of the Law Department, such copy will be held by the recipient for his own reference or destroyed.
When originals of the same or similar correspondence, concerning generally the same subject matter, are directed to several persons, it is not necessary to route the file copy of each piece of correspondence. One file copy may be supplied with the indication thereon that a similar piece of correspondence has been sent to the named persons.

4.34 Internal Correspondence

In the case of a memorandum originating in the Law Department and addressed to another member of the Law Department, a 'show' copy of the memorandum is to be directed to (specify). Such copies will not be circulated or filed.

4.35 Publications

Each publication will be distributed throughout the department in accordance with the route slip attached by the secretary assigned to the mail.
After an attorney has read a particular publication, he or his secretary should cross out his name on the route slip and forward it to the next attorney listed on such slip. It will not be necessary to place an attorney's symbol on the particular publication indicating that he has read it.

124

If an attorney is out of the office for more than one day or if he is unable for one reason or another to read a particular publication within a reasonable time, the publication should be forwarded to the next attorney listed on the route slip. Since the name of the forwarding attorney will not be crossed out on the route slip, the publication will be returned to him after all the other attorneys on the route slip have read the particular publication.

Any attorney desiring to have his name added to, or deleted from, the route slip of a particular publication should advise the secretary assigned to the mail. As new publications are received in the office, they will be circulated to all attorneys and they will be asked to indicate whether or not they desire to be on the route slip for the particular publication.

The last item on the route slip is 'File' or 'Destroy'. After the names of all attorneys have been crossed out on the circulation slip, the particular publication will be destroyed or returned for filing to the secretary of the attorney responsible for the filing of that particular publication in accordance with the filing assignments.

Section V. PROFESSIONAL ACTIVITIES OUTSIDE COMPANY

5.10 Bar Associations

5.11 Memberships
Membership in the Bar Association is encouraged for all attorneys in the Law Department. The company will pay dues for (specify).

5.12 Participation
Each attorney is encouraged to join sections and committees within the bar associations to which he belongs, in order to benefit himself, the company, and the bar association. Diversity between the various sections and committees is encouraged.

5.13 Travel Allowances
The company will pay the costs of attending bar association meetings, and attendance at meetings of sections and committees thereof.

5.14 Publicity
When appropriate, the company may wish to publicize the fact that its attorneys hold memberships in the various bar associations.

5.20 Continuing Legal Education

Attendance at special seminars and programs is encouraged. Company attorneys will be encouraged to participate in such programs. Arrangements and procedures for participating in such programs are described below.

5.21 Approvals

5.22 Expenses

5.23 Arrangements

Section VI. MISCELLANEOUS ADMINISTRATIVE POLICIES

6.10 Library

Maintenance of the library will be the responsibility of a member of the legal staff designated as the librarian by the General Counsel. It will be his responsibility to see that the library is arranged to facilitate efficient use thereof and to insure that the books are maintained in good order.

Library books are not lent to lawyers or others not associated with the company.

Whenever books are removed from the contral library and taken to an attorney's office, a white card provided for that purpose with the attorney's name thereon should be inserted in place of the book removed.

All books and other materials in the library shall be replaced in their proper place when the attorney has finished using them.

6.11 Services, Manuals and Form Books

These should be kept in a centralized location with their access available to all. The various members of the Law Department should be familiar with the various manuals concerning the areas in which they work. One or more secretaries designated by the librarian shall be given responsibility to see that all service and form books are updated as the various changes are received from the publishers. It should also be her responsibility to see that the various services, manuals and form books are kept in their proper place.

6.12 Approval of Library Purchases

The librarian shall give prior approval of all purchases of materials for the library and shall inspect all incoming books, periodicals, and other materials prior to authorizing payment of any invoice.

6.13 Index and Catalog of Materials

A complete index and catalog of all library material is maintained in the library.

Section VII. HANDLING OF CONFIDENTIAL MATERIAL

7.10 Confidential Material

All matters handled by the Law Department are of confidential nature. There should be no discussion of any file except with other members of the legal staff, outside counsel, and other employees of the company having an interest in the matter.

7.11 Handling

All file materials will be kept in the file and will not be removed except when necessary. Exhibits or other materials which are too bulky to be stored in the file will be carefully marked and kept in a designated safe place in the office, and an appropriate notation of their location will be made in the file.

7.12 Disposition

All materials removed from the file will be thoroughly torn up or shredded, and each lawyer will instruct his secretary so tear up all papers she places in a wastebasket. All exhibits will be returned to their original source at the time a file is closed.

VII. Selected Bibliography

'THE ADMINISTRATIVE OFFICE of the United States Courts and Juridicial Counsel of the Second Circuit', The New York Times May 18, 1977.

'ADVOCATS D'EUROPE', Liège, 1977.

AKESON, B., 'Considération sur le Statut et le Rôle du Juriste d'Entreprise en Suède', Le Juriste d'Entreprise, pp. 173-182.

ANSHEN, Melvin, 'Businessmen, Lawyers and Economists: How can they reconcile their Differences and Work together?', Harvard Business Review March-April 1957, pp. 107-114.

APSEY, Lawrence S., 'Organization of a Corporate Legal Department', The Business Lawyer July 1959, pp. 944-956.

ARTHUR, Robert S., 'The Computer and the Practice of Law: Litigation Support', American Bar Association Journal December 1977, p. 1737.

AUSTERN, Thomas H., 'Corporate Counsel Communication: Is Anybody Listening?', The Business Lawyer July 1962, pp. 868-876.

BAERLE, Adolf A., 'The Changing Role of the Corporation and its Counsel', Record of the Association of the Bar of the City of New York, 1955, pp. 266-278.

BAUDOIN, P., 'Het werkterrein van juristen', Nijmegen, 1974 (doctoraal scriptie).

BERG, J.W.M. van den, 'De Bedrijfsjurist', September 1975, mimeographed.

BERNSTEIN, Peter W., 'The Wall Street Lawyers are striving on Change', Fortune March 13, 1978, pp. 104-112.

BINGER, J.H., 'What I Expect from the Ideal Corporate Counsel', The Business Lawyer April 1966, pp. 836-842.

BLOU, Peter M. and SCOTT, B. Richard, 'Formal Organizations: A comparative Approach', 1962.

BÖRTZLER, Fritz, 'Der Syndikusanwalt', Ehrengabe für Bruno Heusinger, München 1968, pp. 119-140.

BOSSARD, J.C., 'De Bedrijfsjurist, Zijn taak en plaats in de onderneming', Ter Kennismaking, January 1972 pp. 17-25.

BROWN, F.F. and JENSEN, W., 'The Lawyer's Role in successful Corporate Enterprise', Business Review April-June, 1962.

BROWN, James K. and FORMAN, Lewis W., 'Board Chairmen, Presidents, Legal Counsel: Some Aspects of Their Jobs', The Conference Board Record January 1967, pp. 9-12.

127

BROWN, James K. and CORMAN, R.E., 'Legal Organization in the Manufacturing Corporation', The Conference Board Record August 1969, pp. 42-47.

BROWN, William E., 'The Professional Change To House Counsel', 28, Notre Dame Lawyer Spring 1953, pp. 333-350.

BUTTS, John D. de, 'The Client's View of the Lawyer's Proper Role', The Business Lawyer, March 1978, pp. 1177-1185.

CANTOR, Daniel J., 'Law Firms are Getting Bigger . . . and More Complex', American Bar Association Journal February 1978, pp. 215-219.

CARSON, Ralph M., 'Privilege and the Work-Product Rule in Corporate Law Departments', The Business Lawyer April 1959, pp. 771-781.

CARTON DE TOURNAI, R., 'Les responsabilités du juriste d'entreprise dans la Société', Journal des Tribunaux, 13 janvier 1968, pp. 17-24.

CHOKA, Allen D., 'The Effective Legal Department: A Primer of Results Oriented Planning', The Business Lawyer April 1969, pp. 825-845.

CHOKA, Allen D., 'The Role of Corporate Counsel', The Business Lawyer April 1970, pp. 1011-1026.

CHURCHILL-ROGERS, 'The Lawyers as Life Company Executive', 24 Tennessee Law Review 1957, pp. 1124-1136.

COMMITTEE REPORT: 'Use of Letterheads by Corporate Law Departments', The Record of the Association of the Bar of the City of New York, December 1977, pp. 680-681.

THE NATIONAL INDUSTRIAL CONFERENCE BOARD, Studies in Business Policy, no. 39, 'Corporate Legal Department', 17, 1950.

THE NATIONAL INDUSTRIAL CONFERENCE BOARD, Business Record, October 1959, 'Organization for Legal Work', pp. 463-468.

THE NATIONAL INDUSTRIAL CONFERENCE BOARD, 'The Legal-Secretarial Function, Top Management Organization in Divisionalized Companies', Studies in Personnal Policy Nr. 195 (1965), pp. 63-67.

THE CONFERENCE BOARD, 'Legal Organization in the Manufacturing Corporation', The Conference Board Record August 1969, pp. 42-47.

COUNCIL OF THE INTERNATIONAL BAR ASSOCIATION, 'A Practical Guide to the Conduct of Lawyer Directors', International Bar Journal May 1978, pp. 33-40.

CREIGHTON, J.R., 'Comment utiliser plus efficacement le conseil juridique ou le service juridique de l'entreprise', Le Juriste d'Entreprise, pp. 229-241.

CREIGHTON, Joseph R., 'Corporate Law Department Adjust to Corporate Decentralization', The Business Lawyer July 1961, pp. 1004-1013.

CREIGHTON, Joseph R., 'Corporate Counsel and Antitrust', American Bar Association Journal July 1962, pp. 654-656.

CRICHTON-MILLER, Neil, 'Job Scope: Lawyers in Business', Sunday Telegraph April 30, 1978.

CUMMINS, William S., 'Status of Corporate Counsel Today', The Business Lawyer July 1966, pp. 1082-1084.

DAVIS, Stephen E., 'House Counsel: The Lawyer with a single Client', American Bar Association Journal September 1955, 830 ff.

DAVIS, Stephen E., 'Corporate Law Department – A New Look at the "New Look"', The Business Lawyer January 1963, pp. 569-571.

DAVIS, Walker B., 'Reflections of a Kept Lawyer', American Bar Association Journal April 1967, pp. 349-353.

DELEUZE, J.M., 'La Prise de décision et l'évolution du role du juriste d'entreprise', Bulletin de l'Association Belge des Juriste d'Entreprise 1970, pp. 56-63.

DEL MARMOL, Charley and Dabin, Léon, 'L'Apport des juristes à la solution des problèmes de la gestion des affaires', Commission Droit et Vie des Affaires, Faculté de Droit de l'Université de Liège, 1963.

DEMAY, M. and RIVERO, M., 'L'Entreprise et le Juriste', Patronat Français No. 26, August-September 1967, pp. 6-11.

DEYMES, Louis M., 'Le Service juridique dans une Entreprise industrielle et commerciale. Ce que l'on attend de lui et l' "Equilibre Mental" qu'il droit acquérir pour y répondre', Le Juriste d'Entreprise, pp. 253-259.

DONNELL, John D., 'The Corporate Counsel', A Role Study, Indiana University, 1970.

DONNELL, John D., 'Reflections of Corporate Counsel In a Two-Way Mirror', The Business Lawyer July 1967, pp. 991-1008.

DRION, T., WOLF, MM.A.L. de, JITTA. J.W.J., KOOMANS, L.J.H., ROGMANS, B.G.P., 'La Fonction et la Position du Juriste d'Entreprise Néerlandais', Le Juriste d'Entreprise, pp. 157-172.

EDWARDS, Clifford W.R., 'Industry's Use of the Lawyer in England', The Business Lawyer November 1960, pp. 124-133.

ETHICAL CONSIDERATION 8-5 of the Code of Professional Responsibility of the American Bar Association, adopted in August 1969.

ETHICAL RESPONSIBILITIES of Corporate Lawyers, The Business Lawyer, Special Issue March 1978, pp. 1453-1475.

FLAMME, Maurice-André 'Le Rôle et les Fonctions du Juriste d'Entreprise', Le Juriste d'Entreprise, pp. 27-47.

'LA FONCTION DU JURISTE d'Entreprise au Grande-Duché de Luxembourg', par La Délégation luxembourgeoise, Le Juriste d'Entreprise, pp. 151-155.

'LA FONCTION DU JURISTE d'Entreprise en Belgique', Le Juriste d'Entreprise, pp. 49-81.

'LA FONCTION DU JURISTE d'Entreprise en Italie', par le Groupe de Travail italien, Le Juriste d'Entreprise, pp. 145-149.

FORSTHOFF, Ernst, 'Der Jurist in der industriellen Gesellschaft', Neue Juristische Wochenschrift 1960, 1273-1277.

FREY, Donald N., 'A Businessman's View of Lawyers', The Business Lawyer January 1978, pp. 817-845.

FRIEDLÄNDER, Adolf und Max, 'Kommentar zur Rechtsanwaltsordnung vom 1. Juli 1878', 3. Auflage 1930.

FROEHLICH, Wolfgang, 'Le Statut du Juriste d'Entreprise en République Fédérale d'Allemagne', Le Juriste d'Entreprise, pp. 91-101.

FULD, James J., 'Legal Opinions in Business Transactions – An Attempt to Bring some Order out of Some Chaos', The Business Lawyer April 1973, pp. 915-945.

GALLI, Fabio, 'In ditta è la legge il mio mestiere',, Espansione November 1977, pp. 100-102.

GAUDET, M. Michel, 'Les juristes d'entreprise et la CEE', Bulletin No. 3, Oct. 1969, Association Belge des Juristes d'Entreprise.

GAVIN, Austin, 'The Educational Function of a Corporate Legal Department', The Business Lawyer January 1961, pp. 370-376.

GERLACH, Dr. Rolf, 'Wirtschaftsjurist', 3. Auflage 1976.

GIBSON, W. David, 'Business of more Lawyers is Business', Chemical Week July 26, 1978, pp. 34-35.

GIJSSELS, Dr. Jan, 'De jurist in de internationale organisaties en in de bedrijven', Rechtskundig Weekblad 1970, pp. 1135-1140.

GIJSSELS, Dr. Jan, 'De advocatuur en het bedrijfsleven', Ars Aequi 1970, pp. 250-256.

GILBERT, Phil E., 'A Joint Responsibility: Corporate Counsel and Retained Counsel', American Bar Association Journal August 1956, pp. 715-719.

GLOOR, Dr. Max, 'Der Jurist im Wirtschaftsleben', Schweizerische Juristen-Zeitung, April 1963, Nr. 7 und 8.

GOLDSTEIN, Tom, 'Job Prospects for Young Lawyers Dim as Fields Grows Overcrowded', The New York Times May 17, 1977.

GOLDSTEIN, Tom, 'A Dramatic Rise in Lawsuits and Costs Concerns Bar', New York Times May 18, 1977.

GOSSETT, William T., 'The Role of the Corporation Counsel', Washington and Lee Law Review 1956, pp. 129-144.

GOULDEN, Joseph C., 'The Superlawyers', New York 1972.

GOW, M.H., 'The Ethics of the Company Lawyer', Le Juriste d'Entreprise, pp. 439-445.

GRAHAME, Orville F., 'What Is Expected of a Corporate Law Department?' American Bar Association Journal February 1963, pp. 159-161.

HAIGHT, James T., 'Keeping The Privilege Inside the Corporation', The Business Lawyer January 1963, pp. 551-561.

HANAWAY, William L., 'Corporate Law Department – A New Look', The Business Lawyer April 1962, pp. 595-602.

HEINTZ, Bruce D., 'The Administrator in the Larger Firm', Legal Economics, Summer 1978., pp. 31-33.

HERSHMAN, Mendes, 'Special Problems of Inside Counsel for Financial Institutions', The Business Lawyer, Special Issue, March 1978, pp. 1435-1448.

HICKMAN, Leon E., 'The Emerging Role of the Corporate Counsel', The Business Lawyer April 1957, pp. 216-228.

HICKMAN, Leon E., 'Corporate Counsel and the Bar', The Business Lawyer July 1959, pp. 925-943.

HICKMAN, Leon E., 'The Need and Utilization of Retained Counsel', Proceedings of Wisconsins Fifth Annual House Counsel Institute, 1969.

HICKMAN, Leon E., 'Corporate Legal Departments re-visited', New York Bar Journal October 1971, pp. 391-393.

HICKS, Lawrence E., 'The Manager and the Law: Using Legal Counsel', Manager's Forum, May 1975.

HILDEBRANDT, Bradford W., 'Managing the Small or Medium Law Office', Practising Law Institute, New York City 1976.

HILDEBRANDT, Bradford W., 'Law Office Economics and Management', Practising Law Institute, New York City 1977.

HILL, John W., 'Corporation Lawyers and Public Relations Counsel', The Business Lawyer April 1959, pp. 587-603.

HOCHBERGER, Ruth, 'Do it yourself is Industry's Reply to Rising Legal Cost', New York Law Journal, Dec. 20, 1976.

HÖHN, Prof. Dr. Reinhard, 'Die "Stabsoffiziere" dürfen keine Manager zweiter Klasse sein', Handelsblatt 30. 5. 1978.

HOFFMANN, Paul, 'Lions in the Street', (The Inside Story of the Great Wall Street Law Firms), 1973.

HOLLIS, E.L., 'What I Expect from a Corporate Client', The Business Lawyer April 1966, pp. 842-847.

HOPSON, Dan jr., And JOHNSTONE, Quintin, 'Corporate Law Departments', Lawyers and Their Work, 1967.

HUNT, Thomas R., 'Corporate Law Department Communication-Privilege and Discovery', Vanderbilt Law Review, 1959, pp. 287-309.

HYATT, Robert R., 'Of House Counsel', The Practical Lawyer May 1957, pp. 73-81.

JOHNSON, James J., 'The Foreign Offices of American Law Firms', Unpublished paper delivered at the American Branch of the International Law Association, New York, April 12, 1978.

JURIS, Juristisches Informationssystem, Beilage 18/1978 des Bundesanzeigers, August 1st, 1978.

'LE JURISTE D'ENTREPRISE', XXe Séminaire de la Commission Droit et Vie des Affaires, Congrès International à Liège du 13 au 16 Décembre 1967, published by the Université de Liège, 1968.

KAIMAN, Stan C., 'Corporate Legal Services: A Primer', The Business Lawyer April 1971, pp. 1131-1144.

KALSBACH, Werner, 'Bundesrechtsanwaltsordnung und Richtlinien für die Ausübung des Rechtsanwaltsberufes', Kommentar, Köln 1960.

KEIR, James D., 'The Role of House Counsel', Company Lawyer's Conference 1977, London.

KERR, James H. jr., 'Developments in Corporate Law', The Business Lawyer July 1963, pp. 917-929.

KIECHEL, Walter, 'The Soggy Case Against the Cereal Industry', Fortune April 10, 1978.

KIECHEL, Walter, 'The Stange Case of Kodak's Lawyers', Fortune May 8, 1978.

KIECHEL, Walter, 'Growing Up at Kutak Rock & Hule', Fortune Oktober 23, 1978.

KNIGHT, Andrew Hendrix, 'The Handling of Legal Matters of a Corporation by its own Law Department', Alabama Law Review 119 (Fall 1959), pp. 119-139.

KOLVENBACH, Dr. Walter, 'Organization of Legal Departments in Larger Corporations with Special Consideration of Inside/Outside Counsel', International Legal Practitioner, May 1977, pp. 10-19.

KOLVENBACH, Dr. Walter, 'Die Organisation von Rechtsabteilungen in Grossunternehmen unter besonderer Berücksichtigung der Beziehungen zwischen interner und externer Rechts-Beratung', Österreichisches Anwaltsblatt Mai 1977, pp. 195-199.

KOLVENBACH, Dr. Walter, 'Dahili ve harici danismaya özel bir bakisla büyük korporasyonlarda hukuk subelerinin örgütlenmesi', Ekonomik Hukuk Dergisi 2/77, pp. 15-24 (Translation by Dr. A. Can Tuncay).

LANAUZE, Jean de, 'De la bonne utilisation des conseils par leurs clients', Cahiers de Droits de l'Entreprise, No. 3, 1976, pp. 1-5.

LAW OFFICE AUTOMATION, Teletext Communication Corp., 1977.

LAW OFFICE EFFICIENCY, American Bar Association and Canadian Bar Association, 1972.

LAW PRACTICE IN A CORPORATE LAW DEPARTMENT, American Bar Association 1971.

THE LAWYER-CLIENT PRIVILEGE: Its Application to Corporations, the Role of Ethics, and its Possible Curtailment, Cited by Northwestern University Law Review, vol 56, 1961, pp. 235-262.

LE BRUN, J., 'Réflexions sur le role du Juriste', Le Juriste d'Entreprise pp. 261-265.

LEE, Norma S., 'Legal Administrators Plan Annual Meeting in Atlanta', New York Law Journal March 27, 1978, pp. 23 and 31.

LEVY, B.H., 'Corporation Lawyer, . . . saint or sinner. The new role of the lawyer in modern society', New York Chilton, 1961.

MADDOCK, Charles S., 'The Corporation Law Department', Harvard Business Review March-April 1952, pp. 119-136.

MADDOCK, Charles S., 'The Challenge To House Counsel', Le Juriste d'Entreprise 1968, pp. 345-360.

MATHES, Sorrell M. and THOMPSON, G. Clark, 'Organization For Legal Work', Business Record October 1959, pp. 463-468.

MATHYS, M.R., 'Lawyers and Businessmen', Le Juriste d'Entreprise, pp. 337-344.

MAURER, Richard S., 'Privileged Communications and the Corporate Counsel', The Business Lawyer July 1961, pp. 959-983.

MAURER, Richard S., 'Ethical and Legal Problems of the Corporate Counsel in the Rendering of Personal Advice to Company Officers and Employees', The Business Lawyer April 1966, pp. 817-828.

MC CLELLAN, Anthony, 'The Company Legal Department', Journal of Business Law, July 1963, pp. 238-245.

MELLO, Xavier de, 'L'Association Française des Juristes d'Entreprise et le

Juriste d'Entreprise', Conference on October 15, 1977, mimeographed.

MILLER, Marjorie A., 'How 16 Typists do Work Processing for a Law Firm with 126 Attorney's, New York Law Journal, March 22, 1977, p. 2

MURPHY, Robert W., 'The Profile of a General Counsel, His Position and Function in an American Corporation', Le Juriste d'Entreprise, pp. 117-123.

NADER, Ralph and GREEN, Mark, 'Don't Pay Those High Legal Bills', The New York Times Magazine November 20, 1977.

'NOTSTAND', Anwälte in Deutschland, Capital 1o/78, pp. 315-326.

O'BRIEN, F.U.J., 'The Law Department of an Oil Company in London', The Business Lawyer November 1960, pp. 113-123.

OFFICIAL JOURNAL OF THE EUROPEAN COMMUNITIES, 26 March 1977, No. L 78, pp. 17-18.

O'MEARA, Arthur C., 'Organizational Structure, Operation and Administration of a Large Corporate Law Department (25 or more Lawyers)', The Business Lawyer April 1962, pp. 584-594.

O'MEARA, Arthur C., 'Committee on Corporate Law Departments Midyear Report for 1964-1965', The Business Lawyer April 1965, pp. 802-806.

PATTERSON, Burton H., 'A Legal Audit Questionnaire', The Business Lawyer January 1971, pp. 983-996.

PEAK, George W., 'Law Departments in Utility Organizations', Public Utilities Fortnightly November 1957, pp. 762-765.

THE PRACTICAL LAWYER'S, Law Office Management, Manual Nr. 3, 1972.

THE PRACTICAL USE OF COMPUTER TECHNOLOGY IN THE LAW OFFICE, Seventeenth Conference of the International Bar Association in Sidney, Australia, 1978, mimeographed.

PROFESSIONS JUDICIAIRE ET JURIDIQUE, Journal Officiel de la Republique Française, No. 1388, 1974.

PROST, Gerhard, 'Der Jurist in der Wirtschaft', Neue Juristische Wochenschrift 1967, pp. 17-21.

PRUSAK, Leonhard P., 'The Lawyer's Role in Industrial Management', The Business Lawyer July 1962, pp. 1033-1043.

REDLICH, Dean Norman, 'Should a Lawyer cross The Murky Divide?', The Business Lawyer, November 1975, pp. 478-481.

REPORT ON THE REGULATION OF FOREIGN LAWYERS, American Bar Association June 1977, pp. 1-50.

RESPONSIBILITY OF LAWYERS ADVISING MANAGEMENT, Panel Discussion, The Business Lawyer March 1975, pp. 13-40.

RICHBELL, Patrick, 'A Survey of the Function and Position of Company Lawyers in England and Wales', Le Juriste d'Entreprise, pp. 113-115.

ROGERS, D.G. Fletcher, 'The Company Lawyer Etiquette and Ethics', Le Juriste d'Entreprise, pp. 431-438.

ROWE, D., 'The Lawyer in Industry', Times Review of Industry, June 1961.

RUDER, David, S., 'A Suggestion For Increased Use of Corporate Law Departments in Modern Corporations', The Business Lawyer January

1968, pp. 341-363.

RUESCHEMEYER, Dietrich, 'Lawyers and their Society', Cambridge, Mass., 1973.

RUSSELL, Brian, 'A Survey of the Function and Position of Company Lawyers in England and Wales', Le Juriste d'Entreprise, pp. 103-112.

RUST, L. Edmund, 'What the Chief Executive looks for in his Corporate Law Department', The Business Lawyer, January 1978, pp. 811-815.

RYAN, John, 'Costly Counsel: Regulations, Fees Boost Companies' Legal Expenses', The Wall Street Journal April 13, 1978.

SAYN-WITTGENSTEIN, Stanislaus Prinz zu, 'Der Jurist in der Wirtschaft', Jura-Berufsreport 1974/75.

SCHAEFER, F.W. Dietmar, 'The Attorney-Client Privilege in the Modern Business Corporation', The Business Lawyer July 1965, pp. 989-995.

SEAMANS, Frank L., 'Relations between corporate legal departments and outside counsel', The Business Lawyer April 1960, pp. 633-637.

SHANKS, Carrol M., 'The Lawyer in Business, His Opportunities and Contributions', Record of the Association of the Bar of the City of New York 1950, pp. 50-61.

SIMON, David, 'The Attorney-Client Privilege as Applied to Corporations', The Yale Law Journal, 1956, pp. 953-990.

SMIGEL, The Wall Street Lawyer, 1966.

SMITH, Sylvester C., 'The Business Executive, Corporate Counsel and General Practitioner', The Business Lawyer January 1958, pp. 220-229.

SMITH, Sylvester C., 'The Outlook of Corporate Counsel', The Business Lawyer January 1963, pp. 323-336.

SMITH, Sylvester C., 'The Changing Status of Corporate Counsel', New York State Bar Journal February 1963, pp. 9-20.

GRUNDSÄTZE DES ANWALTLICHEN STANDESRECHTS vom 1. August 1977, Richtlinien gem. § 117 II 2 BRAO, Richtlinien der Bundesrechtsanwaltskammer, herausgegeben von der Bundesrechtsanwaltskammer, Bonn 1977.

LE STATUT DU JURISTE D'ENTREPRISE EN FRANCE, Le Juriste d'Entreprise pp. 135-144.

STERNIN, Bernhard, 'A Program for Typing Case Data Automatically', The Practical Lawyer, vol 23-No. 1, 1977, pp. 81-88.

STERNIN, Bernhard, 'A System Method for Recording Documents', The Practical Lawyer, vol. 23-No. 4, June 1977, pp. 61-74.

STRACK, WM. N., 'Attorney – Client Privilege – House Counsel', The Business Lawyer April 1957, pp. 229-256.

SULLIVAN, Lawrence A., 'How to Choose and Use a Lawyer', Harvard Business Review September/October 1957, pp. 61-67.

SZABAD, George M. and GERSEL, Daniel, 'Inside vs Outside Counsel', The Business Lawyer November 1972, pp. 235-251.

TER KENNISMAKING, NGB, January 1972.

THOSE LAWYERS, Time April 10, 1978, pp. 50-55.

VAN REEPINGHEN, Paul, 'Le juriste d'entreprise', Journal des Tribunaux, 5 February 1966, p. 104.

VERHULST, F. 'Le Juriste dans l'industrie', Le Juriste d'Entreprise, pp. 243-252.

VLAEMMINCK, Joseph-H., 'Le droit dans l'entreprise', Annales de Sciences Economiques Appliquées, December 1953, pp. 480-490.

WALSHE, Willoughby Ann, 'New Equipment Digest: Speeding the Paper Flow', New York Law Journal May 24, 1977, p. 4.

WENGLER, Wilhelm, 'Über die Unbeliebtheit der Juristen', Neue Juristische Wochenschrift 1959, pp. 1705-1708.

WILLS, Robert V., 'A Prenuptial Primer', The Practical Lawyer March 1962, pp. 49-62.

WOESTE, Dr. Karl Friedrich, 'Inwieweit ist die juristische Ausbildung als Vorbereitung für eine Tätigkeit in der Wirtschaft geeignet?', Neue Juristische Wochenschrift 1969, pp. 1756-1758.

WOODMAN, H.B., 'What the Executive Expects of the Corporate Law Department', The Business Lawyer April 1958, pp. 461-467.

WORD PROCESSING AND LAW FIRMS, Pennsylvania Law Journal, April 24, 1978, p. 10.

YOUNGMAN, Brian J., 'Organisation and Work of the Legal Department of the National Coal Board in England', International Bar Association Sydney Conference, September 1978, mimeographed.